# The
# FRIENDSHIP
# BOOK

## of Francis Gay

**D. C. THOMSON & CO., LTD.**
London   Glasgow   Manchester   Dundee

# A Thought
# For Each Day
# in 1997

*Friendship is a sheltering tree.*
Samuel Coleridge.

# January

I MUST admit I have never read "Pig-Pen Pete" written by Elbert Hubbard, the American editor, lecturer, and essayist born in 1859, but I am rather taken by this quotation from it:-

"Make two grins grow where there was only a grouch before."

Now wouldn't that make a good New Year's resolution?

By the way, have you noticed how a spontaneous friendly smile is often returned by a previously unsmiling face?

A METHODIST minister in Lancashire sent these few lines which I thought so simple, yet so full of the meaning of friendship:

*No grumbling, no sulking, no feuding, no fighting,*
*But looking and looking for things to delight in!*
*No hating the state of the world every minute,*
*But seeking and finding the beauty that's in it.*
*No worrying and letting your troubles confound you,*
*But laughing and liking the people around you!*

# THE FRIENDSHIP BOOK

## FRIDAY—JANUARY 3.

MAY all that these lines express be true for you all through this New Year.

*Happy New Year! Lightly spoken:*
*Mended be the heart that's broken:*
*Soothed the ache that makes us blue:*
*May the year bring comfort true.*

*Happy New Year! Friendship's greeting*
*Through the day we're oft repeating.*
*May the Lord the strength renew*
*For the tasks that all must do.*

*Happy New Year! But tomorrow*
*Should there follow hours of sorrow,*
*God grant courage to endure*
*Hurts that only faith can cure.*

## SATURDAY—JANUARY 4.

I LIKE this advice from Sir Edmund Hillary, one of the brave team that first climbed Mount Everest: "Aim high — there is little virtue in easy victory."

## SUNDAY—JANUARY 5.

BE ye strong therefore, and let not your hands be weak: for your work shall be rewarded.

Chronicles II 15:7

# THE FRIENDSHIP BOOK

## MONDAY—JANUARY 6.

A YOUNG family I know moved into a village not far away. A few weeks after they had settled in, a sudden blizzard caused the whole area to be without power for several days, and afterwards I asked them how they had managed.

"It was amazing," said John. "When we first moved in, nobody seemed very friendly at all, but as soon as the power went off, everything changed. Neighbours started calling to ask if we needed help, or to offer candles. Later, we all joined in a working party to clear drives and pathways. I tell you, Francis, we've never made so many friends so quickly!"

Isn't it wonderful when community spirit really begins to work — and isn't it a pity that it should take a snowstorm to make it?

## TUESDAY—JANUARY 7.

WHEN the American comedian George Burns was 90 he went to see his doctor, complaining of a sore knee. The doctor told him, "You must expect such things at your age."

"Why?" asked Burns. "The other knee's fine and it's just the same age."

## WEDNESDAY—JANUARY 8.

DID you hear the story of the thief who stole a calendar?

He got 12 months!

GLORY IN THE HIGHEST

# THE FRIENDSHIP BOOK

THURSDAY—JANUARY 9.

I FOUND this prayer, written by Sir Thomas More (1478-1535):

*Lord grant me a holy heart that sees always what is fine and pure and is not frightened at the sight of sin, but creates order wherever it goes.*

*Grant me a heart that knows nothing of boredom, weeping and sighing.*

*Let me not be too concerned with the bothersome thing I call 'myself'.*

*Lord, give me a sense of humour and I will find happiness in life and profit for others.*

Surely these thoughts can still help us today.


FRIDAY—JANUARY 10.

CARTOONS, whether on television or in the newspapers, are meant to entertain. However, occasionally they give pause for thought.

I saw one once about a group of characters having a hilarious time skating on a frozen lake. One falls over, and he is so well wrapped in a great thick coat, scarf and mitts, that he can't get up!

A fellow skater, as he came by, calls out, "Let's pray for a quick thaw!" Another friend says nothing, but instead pushes his fallen friend across the ice to the bank, and safety, where he then helps him to his feet.

Sympathetic words have their place in life, and sometimes it is all we can offer, but if there's a chance of giving a practical helping hand, let's not miss the chance!

# THE FRIENDSHIP BOOK

SATURDAY—JANUARY 11.

I WAS driving along an unfamiliar road one Winter afternoon and feeling none too happy about it. The day was cold, the sky was grey and I would much rather have been sitting by a warm fire.

Then, all at once, I noticed a patch of snowdrops growing by the roadside, their pure white heads nodding bravely in the chill wind. Perhaps they were wild ones growing undisturbed, but I like to think that perhaps years ago some kind soul planted them to give pleasure to others who were passing. At any rate, they lifted the spirits of at least one party of travellers that gloomy day.

It made me think of something said by Helen Keller: "When we do the best we can, we never know what miracle is wrought in our own life, or in the life of another."

SUNDAY—JANUARY 12.

THOU art Peter, and upon this rock I will build my church.

Matthew 16:18

MONDAY—JANUARY 13.

A NOTICE seen outside a Glasgow church:

WANTED INSIDE — TRAINEE CHRISTIANS
ONLY SINNERS NEED APPLY
ALL APPLICANTS WILL BE SUCCESSFUL

HIGH WATER

# THE FRIENDSHIP BOOK

I RECENTLY heard a young boy's description of God and found it not only amusing, but as true a description of our freedom of choice as you can get.

He said, "God tells you you mustn't do things and then He lets you do them if you want to!"

I STOOD by the window one morning watching our tame robin enjoying his breakfast. He trusts me to put out a supply of titbits every day, and should I be a little late, he is either on the back doorstep or perched in a nearby bush urging me with his bright-eyed stare to get a move on.

Having eaten, he then flies up into the tree and sings his song of thanks for a satisfying meal. A few minutes of glorious trills and he's off again, this time to his favourite roost, leaving the future to take care of itself.

Perhaps if we tried to copy that robin and trusted more and worried less, we'd find life a little less anxiety-ridden, especially if we look about us with friendly, open eyes, remembering to sing our thanks when appropriate!

I F life is a comedy to the man who thinks, and a tragedy to the one who feels, it is a victory to all who believe.

Anon.

B

# THE FRIENDSHIP BOOK

FEELING miserable one cold January day, a friend of mine went out into the rain for a break — counting her blessings! She passed a florist's shop, and there on display was a tray of polyanthus of every colour.

She bought six quite cheaply. She came home, then later left one on the step of six housebound people with this poem:

*Though today may seem a grey day*
*And you're burdened down with care,*
*It just happens to be pay day,*
*And I've a little cash to spare.*
*There's a florist very near you,*
*So I sorted out my pence,*
*If this little plant will cheer you*
*Then I've used my commonsense.*

It certainly cheered up the recipients, judging by the appreciative telephone calls she received later.

I HOPE you will stop a little while today to read these words written by Charles Kingsley. You will find them in his much-loved book "The Water Babies": —

"The loveliest fairy in the world and her name is Mrs Doasyouwouldbedoneby."

She is certainly an unusual lady, for she is ageless, and no matter where or in what century she is encountered, she is always lovely, and she sets an example for all who meet her.

# THE FRIENDSHIP BOOK

PEACE I leave with you, my peace I give unto you: not as the world giveth, give I unto you. Let not your heart be troubled, neither let it be afraid.

John 14:27

MONDAY—JANUARY 20.

PERHAPS most of us are familiar with the saying "Laugh and the world laughs with you, weep and you weep alone", but did you know that according to recent research, people are losing the art of laughter and it could have a serious effect on our health?

Apparently in 1930 we laughed on average for 19 minutes each day, but by 1980 it had decreased to six minutes. Children, on the other hand, can see the funny side of things more often and may laugh up to 400 times a day.

By expressing air from the lungs in short bursts of laughter, breathing is quickened and heart beats increased, which achieves as much good as ten minutes on an exercise bike. Laughter, too, has a beneficial effect on our immune system, encouraging the production of white blood cells and increasing our resistance to infection. What a difference it makes to our appearance, too, when we relax our facial muscles!

Laughter really is the best medicine, so why not give yourself a treat? Have a good laugh today — and feel better for it!

# THE FRIENDSHIP BOOK

## TUESDAY—JANUARY 21.

**D**RIVING along the road, I spotted this Wayside Pulpit: "It isn't the hours you put in, but what you put into the hours, that counts."

## WEDNESDAY—JANUARY 22.

**S**OME very comfortably-off friends recently invited the Lady of the House and me to lunch. It was a welcome invitation, as it was a dark, cold January day and all the glitter of Christmas with its festivities was over.

Soon our friends were busy telling us of the plans that they were making for a trip to Cyprus. We enjoyed hearing about it all, but as we drove home through the cold rain we both fell silent.

"I know what we'll do when we get home," said the Lady of the House. "We'll get out our photo albums and look at all our old holiday pictures again." We did this and in the midst of Winter, enjoying tea around the fire, the memories of our happy holidays were a real tonic!

Memory can enrich us at any time — it is one of the most precious of our possessions.

## THURSDAY—JANUARY 23.

**F**EELING discouraged? Tempted to give up? Satchell Paige has this advice for all who despair:

"Never let your head hang down. Never give up and sit down and grieve. *Find another way.*"

# THE FRIENDSHIP BOOK

FRIDAY—JANUARY 24.

I WAS talking to a neighbour at the gate one morning, when two young mothers came by, both looking very happy.

"Tell me the good news then," I asked, always keen to hear a good story.

"We've done it!" exclaimed one. "We've raised all the money we need for the school swimming pool."

"All by yourself?" I enquired.

"Oh no," came the laughing reply. "Everyone helped. It was a real joint effort — parents, teachers, the children themselves — everyone worked together."

It's wonderful what can be achieved when we all pull together, isn't it?


SATURDAY—JANUARY 25.

A GARDENER friend offered his considered opinion on marriage and lasting friendship.

They are both, Peter told us, very much like cultivating beautiful plants. This was his recipe and if we follow his directions, our lives will surely be as delightful as his garden —

"Take two people, allow time for understanding to develop. Nurture with sympathy and kindness. Place in a light and cheerful situation. Handle with care and you will find love will bloom abundantly."

He smiled as he surveyed his colourful potted plants and added, "Treasure what you have grown, for love is the greatest gift of life."

# THE FRIENDSHIP BOOK

BE patient therefore, brethren, unto the coming of the Lord. Behold, the husbandman waiteth for the precious fruit of the earth, and hath long patience for it, until he receive the early and latter rain.

James 5:7

I HAVE been re-reading Mrs Gaskell's "Cranford". It is about the close-knit community of simple God-fearing folk, mainly ladies, in the Cheshire village of Cranford, thrown in upon themselves and intensely interested in their neighbours — in the nicest possible way.

The "genteel poverty" upon which they prided themselves is described with gentle humour like sunshine through rain, and with the infinite compassion the characters have for one another.

Mrs Gaskell writes: "I had often occasion to notice the use that was made of fragments and small opportunities in Cranford: the rose-leaves that were gathered ere they fell to make into pot-pourri for someone who had no garden; the little bundles of lavender flowers sent to strew the drawers of some town-dweller, or to burn in the chamber of some invalid. Things that many would despise, and actions which it seemed scarcely worthwhile to perform, were all attended to in Cranford."

Truly has it been said, "For who hath despised the day of small things?"

# THE FRIENDSHIP BOOK

## HEARSAY

WE may hear some gossip
In our lives today,
Gathering momentum
As it's passed along the way.

Add a bit, or take a bit
It's never quite the same,
But unkind words and idle talk
Can harm an honest name.

If there's something good to say
Proclaim it loud and clear,
But it's not worth repeating
If it brings another's tear.

Dorothy M. Loughran.

IF you share an office, a desk, or even a home with someone else you will have sometimes found your colleagues, friends or loved ones rather irritating. At times like this, when the habits of others are getting you down, think of the following advice — it helps.

Someone once asked his minister how to overcome this particular problem. The simple reply was, "By keeping your eyes off other people's faults and fixing them on your own."

# THE FRIENDSHIP BOOK

## THURSDAY—JANUARY 30.

ONE of our oldest friends had been on a coach holiday in Eire. He was telling me about the Irish people and their particular sense of humour, and recounted an amusing tale.

Their coach had been passing through the village of Ennis when their driver pointed out a sign on the front window of a public house in the main street. It read:—

*If you can't come in —*
 *Smile as you pass by.*
After all — a smile is cheaper than a drink!


## FRIDAY—JANUARY 31.

*DID you make your resolutions,*
 *Did you promise to be good?*
*Did you vow to keep your temper*
 *And do all the things you should?*
*Did you promise to be kinder*
 *To the young and very old?*
*Did you promise not to criticise*
 *And never scoff and scold?*
*Did you break your resolutions,*
 *Did you throw them all away?*
*Though you tried a little harder*
 *To do better every day?*
*Just forget those resolutions*
 *And seek out your guiding star,*
*Remember that you're human,*
 *And God loves you as you are!*

Iris Hesselden.

# February

I LIVE near a lovely old city visited by thousands of tourists every year, who come to admire the beautiful cathedral, the ancient High Street, and the unique architecture.

Nevertheless, I am ashamed to say that I have taken very little notice of its attractions and really have scant knowledge of its history.

Last year the Lady of the House and I thought we would have a stay-at-home holiday, and it was a great success. We booked into a modest hotel in the town, were waited on and cosseted for a week, went on the conducted tours and learned for the first time to appreciate the lovely old city.

What a lot of us go hunting far and wide for joy and happiness, missing all the beauty and contentment on our own doorsteps.


SUNDAY—FEBRUARY 2.

FOR even hereunto were ye called: because Christ also suffered for us, leaving us an example, that ye should follow his steps.

Peter I 2:21

# THE FRIENDSHIP BOOK

## MONDAY—FEBRUARY 3.

"I'VE always taken my pension for granted," said Janet, waiting in the post office queue, "but I've just had a new angle on it from my young grandson."

"How so?" I asked.

"Well, this morning as I was starting to climb the stairs he rushed past me, reaching the top before I'd scarcely mounted the second stair. 'I wish I was your age, and could dash up the stairs like that', I said."

"I wish I was *your* age," he called down, "then I'd have a pension and I wouldn't have to beg Mum for money all the time!"

## TUESDAY—FEBRUARY 4.

HERE is a quotation from Archbishop Desmond Tutu about giving.

He says: "We know that God's arithmetic is somewhat odd. When you subtract by giving away, you get more. When you seek to hoard, somehow you lose out."

## WEDNESDAY—FEBRUARY 5.

THE minister had called unexpectedly and was sitting in the front room chatting to Mrs Wynn when they heard the front door open and Daniel, her ten-year-old son, called out, "That was a near thing. I saw the minister in the street a few minutes ago, but I managed to dodge him!"

TOWERS OF STRENGTH

# THE FRIENDSHIP BOOK

IT was old Mary who taught me to singalonga Big Ben!

"I always do it," she told me. "Whenever I hear the chimes on TV or radio, I'm off. Don't you know the words?"

I confessed I did not, so she sang them to me:

*Lord, through this hour,*
*Be thou my guide,*
*Kept by thy power*
*No foot shall slide.*

Try it yourself next time, and spread the message. Wouldn't it be grand to know the whole country was singing it in unison? What a gladsome sound that would be!

IT is said that people who stammer often sing without problems.

A deck-hand who suffered from an impediment in his speech ran to the Captain one day and started: "P-please s-s-sir . . ."

"For goodness sake, hurry up," replied the Captain irritably, "if you can't say it, sing it!"

The deck-hand took a very long breath and began to sing: "Should auld acquaintance be forgot, and never brought to mind; the first mate's fallen overboard, he's half a mile behind."

It is pleasing to record, in this somewhat improbable tale, that the unfortunate man was safely retrieved after an uncomfortable and soggy half-hour.

# THE FRIENDSHIP BOOK

<u>SATURDAY—FEBRUARY 8.</u>

JANE AUSTEN introduces the subject of marriage in "Pride And Prejudice" with gentle irony: "It is a truth universally acknowledged, that a single man in possession of a fortune must be in want of a wife."

William Cobbett in "Advice To Young Men" wrote: "The things which you ought to desire in a wife are Chastity; Sobriety; Industry; Frugality; Cleanliness; Knowledge of Domestic Affairs; Good Temper; Beauty." A paragon indeed!

David Livingstone wrote fondly to his wife Mary: ". . . You have been a great blessing to me. You attended to my comfort in many, many ways. May God bless you for all your kindnesses . . . I never show all my feelings; but I can say truly my dearest, that I loved you when I married you, and the longer I lived with you, I loved you the better."

Albert Chevalier expressed the sentiment well when he sang:

*We've been together now for forty years,*
*An' it don't seem a day too much,*
*There ain't a lady livin' in the land,*
*As I'd swap for my dear old Dutch.*


<u>SUNDAY—FEBRUARY 9.</u>

WHO shall ascend into the hill of the Lord? or who shall stand in his holy place? He that hath clean hands, and a pure heart; who hath not lifted up his soul unto vanity, nor sworn deceitfully.

Psalms 24:3-4

# THE FRIENDSHIP BOOK

IT is comforting to realise that many of our world leaders have a warm, human side also.

I once read something that George Bush, the former United States President, said:

"We all have something to give. If you know how to read, find someone who can't. If you've got a hammer, find a nail. If you're not hungry, not lonely, not in trouble — seek out someone who is."

Now, there's a thought! If we have something to share, let's share it: —

*It was never loving that emptied the heart,*
*Nor giving that emptied the purse.*


TUESDAY—FEBRUARY 11.

A YOUNG lady confided to her friend that she was engaged to be married to a young man whom she had known for only a short time, and was worried whether or not to tell him that she wore false teeth.

Her friend advised her to marry the man and keep her mouth shut.


WEDNESDAY—FEBRUARY 12.

FRIENDLY words can become golden shafts of sunshine when said with sincerity to those who are lonely and alone, troubled and stressed. A case of speech, not silence, being golden.

As the Proverb says: "A word aptly spoken is like apples of gold in settings of silver."

B

# THE FRIENDSHIP BOOK

THURSDAY—FEBRUARY 13.

I WAS listening to two older men on a park bench having a chat. They seemed to be very disgruntled, pulling the world to pieces!

"Yes, Sam, all the world's crazy, except us," said one earnestly. After a bit he added, "But sometimes when I look at you, I begin to wonder."

Isn't that just like so many of us? We always think we are right and everybody else is wrong — including those nearest and dearest to us!

I suspect that most of us need to show a lot more tolerance of others, don't you? Now, there's something to work on today.

FRIDAY—FEBRUARY 14.

"OH, they're beautiful!" exclaimed the Lady of the House, as I handed over a bunch of red roses I'd bought. "I suppose you know that red roses are the symbol of love?"

"Yes," I said, "that's why I bought them, though I don't know the story behind it all."

"Oh, I can tell you!" she said. "After Adam and Eve were banished from the Garden of Eden, Eve slipped back to pick a rose to show Adam she still loved him. She wanted a red rose, but all she could find was a white one. Then she kissed it, and it turned red. That's why red roses have been exchanged between lovers ever since."

I was glad I'd bought these roses on the way home. If I hadn't, I might never have heard that lovely tale!

C

# THE FRIENDSHIP BOOK

I DON'T know who wrote "What Is A Friend?" but don't you think it sums up perfectly the meaning of friendship?

*A talk when you're lonely,*
*A smile when you're glad,*
*A help when you're weary,*
*A hope when you're sad,*
*A hand when you need it,*
*A laugh when you're blue,*
*A guide when you're searching,*
*A joy all life through.*

THE Lord be between me and thee, and between my seed and thy seed for ever.

Samuel I 20:42

A RUMOUR was going round Oxford that Rudyard Kipling, the poet, was being paid a shilling a word for his writings, so a group of Oxford students thought they would put the matter to the test.

They sent him a shilling piece, together with a message: "Please send us one of your words."

Perhaps they didn't expect to be taken literally, but back came the unexpected answer:— "Thanks".

# THE FRIENDSHIP BOOK

LET me share with you the following lines written by William Morris, the Victorian writer and artist. They come from "The Earthly Paradise", and I find them cheering in the dog days of a long, hard Winter, when it seems Spring is a long time coming:

*Late February days; and now, at last,*
*Might you have thought that Winter's woe was past;*
*So fair the sky was and so soft the air.*

To wake up to such a February day of blue skies and clear, pale sunshine after a succession of cold, grey days is a delightful reminder that Spring is just around the corner. In the same way, a surprise occasion of happiness during any troubled period in our lives reminds us that there is always a turn in the road, and that better times lie ahead.

CHILDREN may find some Bible stories difficult to understand. On the other hand, they may see things which we miss.

A Sunday School teacher was telling the story of the Prodigal Son, and to make sure that the lesson had been well understood, she asked, "In the midst of all the rejoicing for the prodigal's return, there was one for whom the feast brought no joy, but only bitterness. Can you tell me who it was?"

"The fatted calf!" suggested a little voice.

A very logical answer, too, even if it was not quite what the teacher expected.

# THE FRIENDSHIP BOOK

## THURSDAY—FEBRUARY 20.

IN his later years, the late Dr Fisher, former Archbishop of Canterbury, was chairman at an informal session of the first Assembly Of The World Council Of Churches.

One of the younger delegates was somewhat outspoken, and suggested that folk of Dr Fisher's generation were now back numbers.

The Archbishop was equal to the occasion, and interrupted the speaker with a twinkle in his eye, saying, "Maybe, but back numbers are useful for lighting fires."

## FRIDAY—FEBRUARY 21.

FRIENDSHIPS begun in this world will be taken up again, never to be broken off.

St Francis de Sales.

## SATURDAY—FEBRUARY 22.

### YOUNG AT HEART

*IF you're sometimes feeling
that you're really getting old,
Remember every birthday
Has a new age to unfold.
No matter how the years add up,
They do along the way,
Simply think — I don't feel older —
Just a different age today!*

Elizabeth Gozney.

# SPRING CRUISE

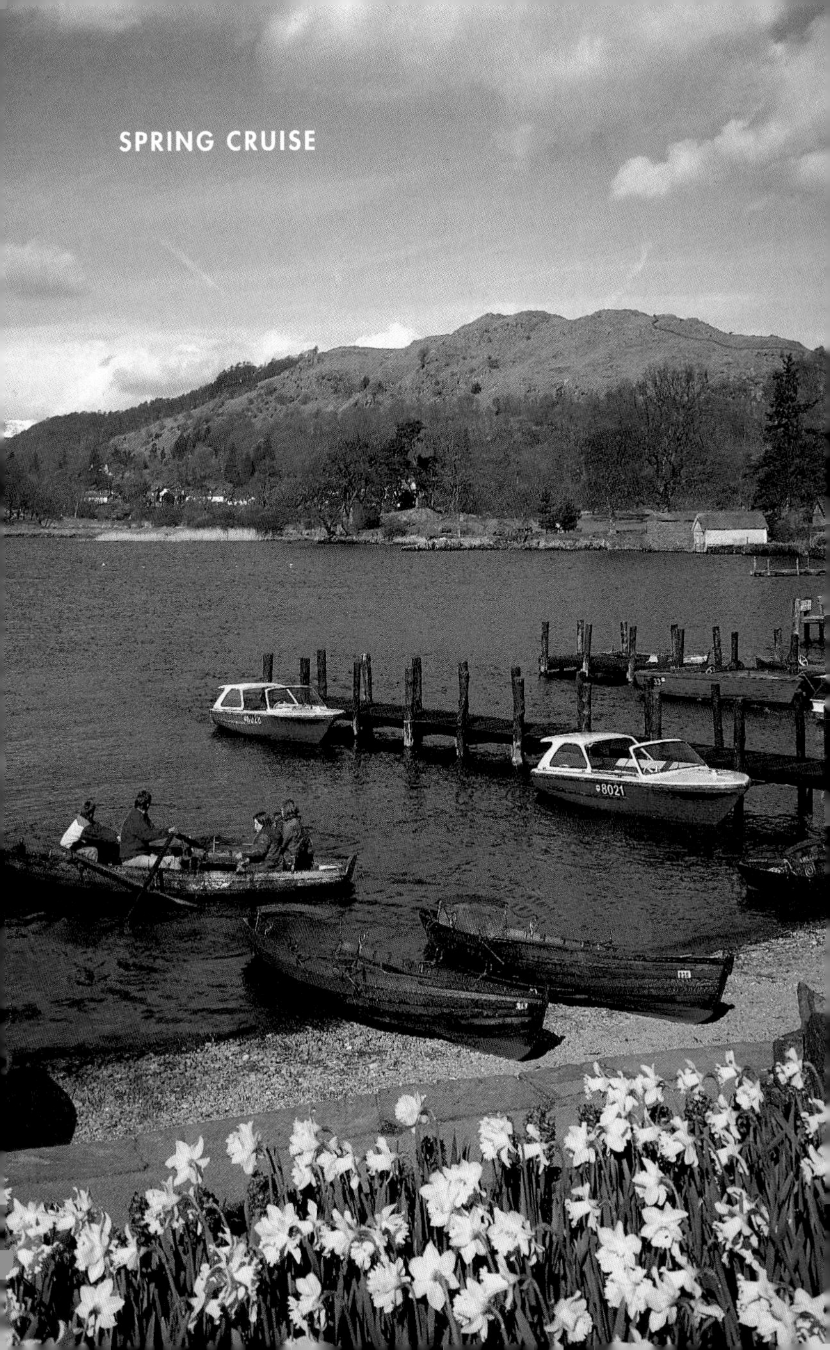

# THE FRIENDSHIP BOOK

SUNDAY—FEBRUARY 23.

THE Lord is my strength and song, and he is become my salvation.

Exodus 15:2

MONDAY—FEBRUARY 24.

A YOUNG man walked into a doctor's surgery one morning and asked the receptionist if he could have an anti-tetanus injection immediately. She asked him why, and he replied that he'd been helping with some renovation work in an old church hall and had suddenly fallen through the floor where the boards were rotten, cutting his leg in the process.

"Oh," she replied, "I've often wished for the floor to open up and let me disappear, after I'd said something I shouldn't have. Had you just said something nasty?"

"No," he replied, "but I did *when* it happened!"

TUESDAY—FEBRUARY 25.

IS there anything more wonderful and full of promise than the dawn of a new morning? The writer Mary Jean Irion used to greet every day with this thought:

"Let me be aware of the treasure you hold. Let me learn from you, love you, savour you, bless you before you depart. Let me not pass you by in quest of some rare and perfect tomorrow."

Amen to that.

# THE FRIENDSHIP BOOK

### WEDNESDAY—FEBRUARY 26.

HERE are two quotations on happiness to ponder today:—

"One thing I know: the only ones among you who will be really happy are those who will have sought and found how to serve others."

(Albert Schweitzer)

"The secret of happiness is not in doing what one likes, but in liking what one has to do."

(J. M. Barrie)

### THURSDAY—FEBRUARY 27.

"NOT another bookmark, Francis!" laughed the Lady of the House. She knows I have a weakness for collecting them, and my excuse is that I always have several books in use at the same time.

But when she saw this one, she understood why I had bought it. It says: — "No act of kindness, no matter how small, is ever wasted."

### FRIDAY—FEBRUARY 28.

THE Sunday school teacher explained that Elijah built an altar, placed wood upon it, cut the sacrificial bullock in pieces and laid them on the wood. He then commanded the people to fill four jars with water, and pour the water over the sacrifice.

"Why do you think they did that?" she asked.

One little girl raised her hand and said, "To make gravy!"

# March

I THINK that roses are the favourite amongst all my flowers, for they give immense pleasure from early June until well into November.

Consequently, I take a lot of care when I prune them, cutting out dead wood and branches that turn inwards or cross one another, in order to allow light and air into the centre of the bush, shortening long stems to increase strength, and generally making the bushes into pleasing shapes. In fact, I do all I can to ensure that they are in the best possible condition to produce fine blooms the following season.

It's good to prune our lives from time to time as well, cutting out any little resentment, envy or strife that mars our relationships. It can make all the difference to the way we feel and will help *us* to bloom, too.

SUNDAY—MARCH 2.

FOR the Lord thy God bringeth thee into a good land, a land of brooks of water, of fountains and depths that spring out of valleys and hills; A land of wheat, and barley, and vines, and fig trees, and pomegranates; a land of oil olive, and honey.

Deuteronomy 8:7-8

# THE FRIENDSHIP BOOK

## MONDAY—MARCH 3.

WHAT a precious thing is content! It can make all the difference to life, can't it?

Here are two old sayings about it which I came upon recently:

"Content is the philosopher's stone; it turns all it touches into gold."

"Content lodges oftener in cottages than in palaces."

## TUESDAY—MARCH 4.

WHEN two old friends were celebrating their 50th wedding anniversary, their young grandson asked if he might have a second piece of the elaborate iced cake. Grandma told him he couldn't, as one was quite sufficient for a small boy, but she added: "If you are still hungry you can have a piece of bread and butter."

"I'm not bread and butter hungry!" came the reply.

What a pity that such a lot of us want the cake of life, but when it comes to the life-giving bread so many are not hungry.

## WEDNESDAY—MARCH 5.

DR CAREY, the Archbishop of Canterbury, once said, "Don't be worried about failing, be a glorious enthusiastic failure rather than a tired and timid traveller on a trouble-free road."

How right he was.

# THE FRIENDSHIP BOOK

<u>THURSDAY—MARCH 6.</u>

THE Lady of the House and I called to see our old friend Mary.

"Come in!" she greeted us cheerily. "I'm cleaning my sitting-room cupboard. It's where I store my photographs, letters, birthday cards and all my special keepsakes. You know, I keep stopping to have another look at them, so the tidying is taking me rather a long time. But what a happy afternoon I've had!"

"That's lovely, Mary," I said, "because it is said that memories live for ever."

"You're quite right," she replied. "We must always cherish our old memories, but we must take care never to forget our young hopes."

As usual, I came away from Mary with something to think about!

<u>FRIDAY—MARCH 7.</u>

SOME years ago I was in Yorkshire visiting choral societies. Some conductors and choir members had amusing, as well as helpful, anecdotes to relate.

The conductor of the prize-winning Hebden Royd Old People's Choir, mentioned that on one occasion his choir came top in a music festival. One of his elderly members later came up to him and said, "Eh, that sounded grand. It were so grand I just had to stop singing to listen to it!"

Amusing, rather than helpful!

# THE FRIENDSHIP BOOK

SATURDAY—MARCH 8.

A FRIEND of mine often does kindnesses for others, but afterwards she spoils her deeds by saying, "Well, now I've got a down payment of goodwill there — a sort of credit note!"

She means, of course, that if she wants something done in the future she will feel free to ask that person for it!

I can't help thinking that is no way to do a favour — thinking only of the "credit" one can gain. Kindness should be spontaneous and without thought of future rewards.

SUNDAY—MARCH 9.

T HIS beginning of miracles did Jesus in Cana of Galilee, and manifested forth his glory; and his disciples believed on him.

John 2:11

MONDAY—MARCH 10.

R ECENTLY, I came across this old proverb which I found rather amusing.

"You can't keep trouble from coming, but you needn't give it a chair to sit on!"

It made me think of people I know who dwell on their troubles so much, that they miss all the sunshine. We all have problems at some time in our lives, but we must remember that when trouble comes knocking, we mustn't encourage it to stay!

A wise proverb indeed.

# THE FRIENDSHIP BOOK

TUESDAY—MARCH 11.

ONCE, on holiday, I was walking in very bright sunshine when I came on an old church. Pushing open the door I went in — and at first couldn't see a thing. I seemed to be staring into total blackness.

Then, as I edged forward, guided by the pews, my eyes grew accustomed to the dark. Gradually I made out the altar, the pulpit, flowers on a table. It all became clear.

It struck me afterwards that this must be how some people find their faith. They come in out of the dark and, little by little, God's purpose and love become clear to them, until at last they are bathed in His wonderful light.

Yes, that old church taught me a lot.

WEDNESDAY—MARCH 12.

"I DON'T want to talk about it, it won't do any good." Our friend Alex had a problem, and couldn't see his way to solving it, but was quite definite he didn't want to discuss it.

Yet I wonder how many misunderstandings have been cleared up, and problems solved or lightened by a little chat? Talking through a problem with a discreet and sympathetic listener can be therapeutic, and can help to put a problem in perspective, even suggest a solution.

I think I agree with Norman Douglas, that cosmopolitan and much-travelled writer, when he said: "Everything is worth talking about."

# THE FRIENDSHIP BOOK

I KNOW a man with a rather strange hobby — he collects epitaphs from old gravestones. It's not such a serious pastime as it sounds. Take this one, for instance:—

*Here lies my wife Polly,*
*A terrible shrew;*
*If I said I was sorry*
*I should lie, too!*

Another man must have had a similar partner because this was his epitaph for his wife —

*Here snug in grave*
*My wife doth lie,*
*Now she's at rest*
*And so am I.*

I LIKE this little verse from the United States which appeared anonymously in a Salvation Army magazine:—

### LENDING A HAND

*A patient ear, a kindly eye,*
*A ready, helping hand,*
*A gentle spirit, and a heart*
*That's quick to understand;*
*With these, in my small corner*
*May I spread joy and light,*
*And take a friendly candle*
*Into someone else's lonely night.*

# THE FRIENDSHIP BOOK

OUR pink-flowered Easter cactus gives us much pleasure when it's in full bloom.

Cacti are interesting plants, striking examples of adaptation to the environment in which they grow in the wild. To survive they have to do without water during long periods of drought, so they have modified their structure to enable them to store rainwater whenever it falls.

We, too, should learn to adapt to circumstances we can't change, instead of wasting energy resenting something that will happen regardless.

The lovely Easter cactus has a valuable message for every one of us — as well as being just a beautiful plant to look at.

PRAISE ye the Lord. Praise the Lord, O my soul.

Psalms 146:1

" HAPPINESS is a habit — cultivate it!"

I was reminded of that good advice when a friend said to me, "Francis, live and enjoy every moment of any happiness that comes your way in life."

If we do, we may find that we have more of those moments of happiness to enjoy than we ever expected or hoped for.

# THE FRIENDSHIP BOOK

<u>TUESDAY—MARCH 18.</u>

IN Malaysia, so I am told, there is a very nice custom of celebrating some aspect of nature with a party. Guests are invited to join in a quiet, contemplative evening such as a moon party, where they are expected to do nothing but relax and enjoy viewing the rising moon. A peaceful way to spend time in an often busy life!

Other opportunities that come to mind are a daybreak party for the early risers, a first day of Spring party, or a fruits of our garden celebration.

Think of all the good things we could celebrate if we really put our mind to it. Whether we choose to do it on our own or in the company of friends, the lovely things around us can provide us with endless excuses for rejoicing.


<u>WEDNESDAY—MARCH 19.</u>

WHEN we are angry or impatient, we are liable to vent our displeasure wherever we go. A light-hearted view of this can be taken with the following sayings I've collected:—

*Had a bone to pick with the butcher;*
*Saw red at the traffic lights;*
*The slater made me hit the roof;*
*The dentist had me grinding my teeth;*
*Gave the psychiatrist a piece of my mind;*
*Had to put my foot down to the chiropodist.*

By the time you've thought about these, their humour may have restored your own!

SAYING IT
WITH FLOWERS

# THE FRIENDSHIP BOOK

THURSDAY—MARCH 20.

WHEN old Miss Martin decided to move from her big old house to a small one in a retirement complex everyone wondered how she would feel about parting with so many of her lovely things — the pictures, the furnishings, the ornaments she loved.

However, for Miss Martin it was no problem at all. I met her the other day and she told me why.

"I gave my favourite things to my friends," she told me. "Mrs Smith has one painting that hung in the drawing-room, Miss Dow has another, then Miss Wilks took the nest of tables and Mr and Mrs Dent were delighted to take some of the ornaments. My friends are all delighted, and so am I! I know my things are in good hands and I still see them if I happen to call."

FRIDAY—MARCH 21.

KATE DOUGLAS WIGGIN, author of the popular children's stories about Rebecca of Sunnybrook Farm, wrote a charming little piece entitled "To My Mother":

"Most of all the other beautiful things in life come by twos and threes, by dozens and hundreds; plenty of roses, stars, sunsets, rainbows, brothers and sisters, aunts and cousins, but only one mother in all the wide world."

I think any mother would take heart from such a tribute, don't you?

D

# THE FRIENDSHIP BOOK

**H**AVE you done your exercises lately?
These days we are told by health and fitness experts to exercise more: "Exercise every day, it will help your muscles and your general health — stretch out your arms and your legs as far as they will go!"

Perhaps some of us forget to do our exercises, until we really begin to feel rheumaticky and stiff. This is a bit like the way we tend to say our prayers, don't you think? We happily miss the habit until a crisis comes along — and then we remember.

So, as I once heard a minister say, "Do your exercises every day; just get down on your knees and put your hands together — that is all that is necessary."

**V**ERILY, verily, I say unto you, If a man keep my saying, he shall never see death.

John 8:51

**H**ERE are a few lines to make you smile — *and think!*

*Every time I pass a church
I pay a little visit,
So when at last I'm carried in,
The Lord won't say, "Who is it?"*

# THE FRIENDSHIP BOOK

HAVE you written any letters lately?
Katherine Mansfield spelled it out: "It really is a heavenly gift to be able to put yourself, jasmine, Summer grass, a kingfisher, a poet, a pony, an excursion, the new sponge-bag and bedroom-slippers into an envelope."

The best letters are of this kind — written from life. Some may be witty, some tender, a few indiscreet perhaps, but personal memories and thoughts never come amiss to the recipient.

Nor do letters of encouragement and affection. The mere sight of familiar handwriting on the envelope can do so much to lift one's spirits in an age when letter-writing is perhaps not as frequent as it used to be.

Have *you* written any letters lately?

ANGELA, aged seven, was staying with her grandparents over Easter and went to church with them on Easter Day. As they left church afterwards, the minister shook hands and asked Angela if she had enjoyed the service. She nodded enthusiastically.

"And what is your favourite hymn?" he continued.

For a moment Angela's brow furrowed as she tried to think of an answer, then her face cleared as she replied triumphantly, "It's 'Thank Heaven For Little Girls'."

# THE FRIENDSHIP BOOK

## THURSDAY—MARCH 27.

I HAVE been reading Chinese proverbs and teachings. They are usually so very old and profound — well worth thinking about seriously, and applying in our own lives today.

I came across this one recently that I had not seen before:

"If there is sufficient mud thrown around — some sticks. If there is sufficient sunshine around — some penetrates."

## FRIDAY—MARCH 28.

I WENT into the back garden one morning to pick up a bag of rubbish which had blown over during the night, shedding its contents. It was a bitterly cold day, with a biting north-east wind that flattened daffodils and tulips and made me think we were back to Winter.

Yet every year, as surely as night follows day, Winter passes. Warm weather returns, we delight again in the loveliness of Spring flowers, and we can look forward with confidence to Summer in full blossom.

I was reminded once more of the Easter story. The events of that first Good Friday brought the greatest of sorrow and despondency. They were followed, however, by Easter Sunday, and the message of Easter — for Christian folk at any rate — is that Christ rose from the dead bringing hope, joy and the promise of new life to all mankind.

A very happy Easter to you all!

PEAK POWER

# THE FRIENDSHIP BOOK

**D**ID you know there is an Easter lichen? I didn't until recently.

Lichens are interesting plants. My gardening friend Peter tells me that in their natural habitats, lichens represent a mutual life-giving partnership between an alga and a fungus, each depending on and co-existing with the other.

The alga gets moisture, protection, and necessary salts in solution, from the fungus. In its turn, the alga makes organic food using its chlorophyll, then supplies this to the fungus.

Co-operation with others can achieve many worthwhile things in life — an Easter message I never imagined I'd be taught by lichen.

**F**OR to this end Christ both died, and rose, and revived, that he might be Lord both of the dead and living.

Romans 14:9

**A** HIGHLAND preacher once embellished the 23rd Psalm with his reference to the faithful sheepdogs: "The Lord is my shepherd. Aye, and more than that: He has two collie dogs, named Goodness and Mercy. With the shepherd before, and them behind, even poor sinners like you and me can hope to win home at the last."

# April

TUCKED away in the grass on the road-side I found a treasure — a small clump of violets. Tiny, unobtrusive flowers, such a contrast to the bright, gleaming gold of daffodils in Spring flower borders.

They made me think how all too easy it is in life to overlook, or forget, the little things than can mean so much — the affectionate hug; the phone-call we promised; the letter to a distant friend or relative; the word of thanks, or praise. Just small gestures of love in life may have greater impact than we can ever imagine.

WEDNESDAY—APRIL 2.

A MAN once saw anglers along a river bank, fishing for salmon. They were trying all they knew to hook the fish, but the salmon just kept leaping and rolling in the air, shining like silver in the sunshine.

He could not help thinking what a carefree life those salmon had. All they had to do to stay happy and carefree was: *keep their mouths shut.*

Not bad advice to the provoked, is it?

# THE FRIENDSHIP BOOK

## THURSDAY—APRIL 3.

IT isn't surprising that one of our greatest poets, William Wordsworth, should be so moved by the beauty of a field of daffodils that he became inspired to write those famous lines: —

*And then my heart with pleasure fills,*
*And dances with the daffodils.*

I defy anyone to look on a mass display of these lovely golden blooms and not feel uplifted. It's not only their magnificence, of course, it is above all, the joyous sign that it is now Spring, a time of re-awakening.

Bless you, noble daffodil, for your message of hope. You're not the most practical of plants — you can't be eaten, you have next to no scent, and your stems are brittle, but what does all that matter? You give us such joy, such a sense of wonder, just looking at you.

Enjoy the months of sleep you'll soon be starting, precious yellow flowers. And next year, come back again to brighten our days.

## FRIDAY—APRIL 4.

SOME of the old proverbs contain a great deal of good advice in just a few words. All the same, I must confess to preferring this modern variation of an old one.

"Never put off till tomorrow what you can do today. For if you have enjoyed what you have done today, you can do it again tomorrow!"

# THE FRIENDSHIP BOOK

ONE birthday I was given a most attractive weekly diary. The illustrations were truly inspirational in their beauty, but I looked at the seven, neatly-ruled lines alongside in some dismay — seven lines, seven days, waiting for me to write on them the events in my daily life.

These events are so mundane, though, that it seemed an insult to write beside the magnificent pictures "Dentist", "Car For Service", "Plumber", etc. They deserved something better.

Then I had an idea — I'd keep a Thanks Diary. Each day, without fail, I'd jot down at least one thing, no matter how small, to be thankful for.

It became a challenge as the days went by, because I found myself repeating things. That didn't matter — the important thing was to keep it going, and keep it going I did.

Now my diary is something to keep forever, to browse through over and over again. I've created a Book of Thankfulness and Memories — and I'd like to pass my idea on to you, hoping you will take up the challenge yourself.

THINE, O Lord, is the greatness, and the power, and the glory, and the victory, and the majesty: for all that is in the heaven and in the earth is thine, thine is the kingdom, O Lord, and thou art exalted as head above all.

Chronicles I 29:11

# THE FRIENDSHIP BOOK

MONDAY—APRIL 7.

I WAS walking along the road with young Emily when we came across a puddle into which some petrol had been spilled, making a series of lovely colours.

"Oh, look," she exclaimed, "somebody has dropped a rainbow!"

I couldn't help thinking how much better a place the world would be if more of us saw a discarded "rainbow" among the ordinary happenings of life.

TUESDAY—APRIL 8.

I HAVE just come across a splendid French proverb which translated reads: "Write injuries in sand, kindness in marble."

What a sound idea — injuries, slights, resentments are all ugly things that sour our minds and hearts. Treat them as sand which is quickly blown away. Kindness, of word or deed, is worth remembering — and marble endures forever.

WEDNESDAY—APRIL 9.

### GET WELL!

*B EEN feeling under the weather?*
*Then hoping very soon,*
*You'll be feeling on top of the world again,*
*If not quite over the moon!*
                    Elizabeth Gozney.

# THE FRIENDSHIP BOOK

## THURSDAY—APRIL 10.

THE Lady of the House and I like to encourage birds to come to our garden, and so we supply them with food and water during the Winter months.

We were particularly pleased when a pair of blackbirds decided that the thick honeysuckle on our fence was the ideal place to build a nest and raise a family. They became so secure in our presence that they pecked around our feet when we ate outside, and fluttered only a few inches away when we walked nearby.

What precious things security and trust are — within marriage and family life, between friends, teacher and pupil, or doctor and patient. It takes time to build up that sort of relationship, but trust is a two-way street and once we get there, let's do all we can to keep the traffic flowing!

## FRIDAY—APRIL 11.

DURING the dark days of the Second World War, people in Britain kept their spirits up singing popular songs that were full of hope. Who can forget these lines, for instance?

*There'll be bluebirds over*
*The white cliffs of Dover . . .*

My own favourite, though, was this one (and I still sing it in the bath!):

*It's a lovely day tomorrow,*
*Tomorrow is a lovely day . . .*

Now, there's pure optimism for you!

NATURE'S
PAINTBRUSH

# THE FRIENDSHIP BOOK

SATURDAY—APRIL 12.

THE members of the Emsworth branch of the Mother's Union near Portsmouth offer a helping hand to people who have had to go into hospital unexpectedly.

The idea was sparked off when they heard of a lady who broke her arm while out shopping, and was whisked into hospital straight away. As she lived alone and her family was not nearby, she had nobody to bring her basic necessities. With the help of donations, the Mothers' Union ladies provided an initial dozen bags of toiletries for further emergencies, containing soap, a flannel, toothbrush and small towel, all accompanied by a complimentary M.U. card. They were delivered to the Queen Alexandra's Hospital, Portsmouth.

Later, a commercial organisation donated 100 tubes of toothpaste and more bags were prepared, the more recent ones containing in addition shampoo and a comb. Many hospital patients have since benefited from the project.

The blue and white enamel badge of the Mothers' Union consists of a monogram of the entwined letters M.U. It has been described as "M for me, supporting U for you" — an apt description indeed of the Emsworth Ladies' project.

SUNDAY—APRIL 13.

AND thou shalt go to thy fathers in peace; thou shalt be buried in a good old age.

Genesis 15:15

# THE FRIENDSHIP BOOK

## MONDAY—APRIL 14.

OLD Mrs Bradshaw was bemoaning the fact that her sponge cakes never won a prize in the competitions.

"I always put in the very best ingredients, too, Francis," she said.

I pointed out to her that it was like life. Many people put all their energies and "best ingredients" into some project, only to find that it doesn't come up to their great expectations. The only thing to do is to keep trying and, even if you never reach your desired goal, the effort in itself is rewarding.

"It is better to travel hopefully than to arrive."

## TUESDAY—APRIL 15.

IN 1845 Henry David Thoreau, the American natural history writer, built a little cabin in which to live. He was seeking a simple lifestyle, which would enable him to devote his time to writing and observing nature.

His words: "Our life is frittered away by detail. Simply simplify", are ones to remember when our lives become rather too busy and stressful, and things seem to be getting on top of us.

## WEDNESDAY—APRIL 16.

I RATHER like what Augustine Birrell has to say of friendship in his "Obiter Dicta":

"Friendship is a word the very sight of which in print makes the heart warm."

# THE FRIENDSHIP BOOK

THOMAS EDISON was one of the world's greatest inventors, and he was great in character, too, as this story demonstrates. When he was working on improvements to his light bulb, he handed a finished bulb to a young assistant, who nervously carried it upstairs, step by careful step. At the last moment . . . he dropped it!

The whole team had to work another two days to make another bulb. When it was ready, Edison looked across the workroom and handed it to the *same* boy, a gesture which undoubtedly not only made an impression, but also changed that boy's life.

The astute Edison knew that more than the bulb was at stake.

THE music of life is for you and for me,
It plays in the mountains, it sings in the sea.
It whispers at harvest time, stirring the grain,
It beats on the windows and drums in the rain.
The high and the low notes, the good and the bad,
All blending together, both happy and sad.
Our youth is the overture, life just begun,
A fanfare of trumpets, a hymn to the sun.
The music grows stronger, a song meant to last,
Composed of the future, the present, the past.
A melody timeless, eternally new,
The music of life is for me and for you.

Iris Hesselden.

# THE FRIENDSHIP BOOK

IF ever I find difficulty in sleeping, I think about the Rev. Hilary Eliot, one of the characters in Elizabeth Goudge's novel, "The Heart Of The Family". He was a man of deep faith and this led him to look for blessings in situations where many of us might not find it easy to do so.

I quote: "Hilary smoothed out the crumpled pages of his sermon, folded it and put it deep in his pocket. He sometimes thought what a merciful thing it was that his rheumatism so often kept him awake at night. In the small hours he could accomplish so many things which somehow or other he could never find time to do during the day."

It may take a bit of practice, but as my grandmother often used to say, "If life gives you a lemon, the only thing to do is to make lemonade."

IN thee, O Lord, do I put my trust; let me never be ashamed: deliver me in thy righteousness.

Psalms 31:1

I LIKE the story of the Sunday school class which was studying the parable of the Wise and Foolish Virgins. The scholars were all girls, and their teacher asked them what the parable was meant to teach.

Quick as a flash came the reply: "Please, miss, to be always on the look-out for a bridegroom!"

BLUE HAVEN

# THE FRIENDSHIP BOOK

<u>TUESDAY—APRIL 22.</u>

THIS charming old Gaelic blessing was sent to me by Mrs Jeannie Peck of Louth. She lives far from Gaeldom, in Lincolnshire, but the words are universal as I hope you'll agree when you read on: —

*Deep peace of the running wave to you*
*Deep peace of the flowing air to you*
*Deep peace of the quiet earth to you*
*Deep peace of the shining stars to you*
*Deep peace of the Prince of Peace to you*

*May the road rise to meet you*
*May the wind be always at your back*
*May the sun shine warm upon your face*
*May the rains fall softly upon your fields*
*Until we meet again may God hold you*
*in the hollow of his hand.*

What a lovely idea!


<u>WEDNESDAY—APRIL 23.</u>

ON one occasion I visited York Old Priory Choir. This had its monthly publication called "The Bulletin" edited by Mrs G.M. Terry.

In the issue of April 1968 she relates how an old man who was always smiling was asked what made him so cheerful. After all, his life was not so easy — in fact, he had experienced much hardship.

He just smiled wider than ever and remarked, "That's simple. I co-operate with the inevitable."

Still a good lesson to keep in mind!

# THE FRIENDSHIP BOOK

## THURSDAY—APRIL 24.

SOME time ago I was asked to collect for one of the many charities. Delivering the small coloured envelopes was no trouble at all, but I set out to collect them at the end of the week with some trepidation. Some people had recently been made redundant and I wondered how folk would react.

I got a great surprise! At each door I was received with encouragement and pleasantness. Even the few who could not give, explained this with a kindly word and a smile.

I was surprised to find generosity in many unexpected places. My faith has now been enriched.

## FRIDAY—APRIL 25.

A FRENCH soldier was captured by the Saracens during the Crusades. As he lay in prison in chains he prayed for his release, and made a vow that if he ever returned home he would suspend a symbolic chain between the cliffs behind the village of Moustiers he loved so well.

He was freed and, true to his word, had the chain put up, linking one cliff with another. By the end of last century the chain was decayed so a new one was hung, this time adorned with a bright star in the middle.

If ever you visit Moustiers, in Provence, you will see it there, suspended high above a tiny church on the edge of the gorge, the symbol of a man's gratitude for an answered prayer.

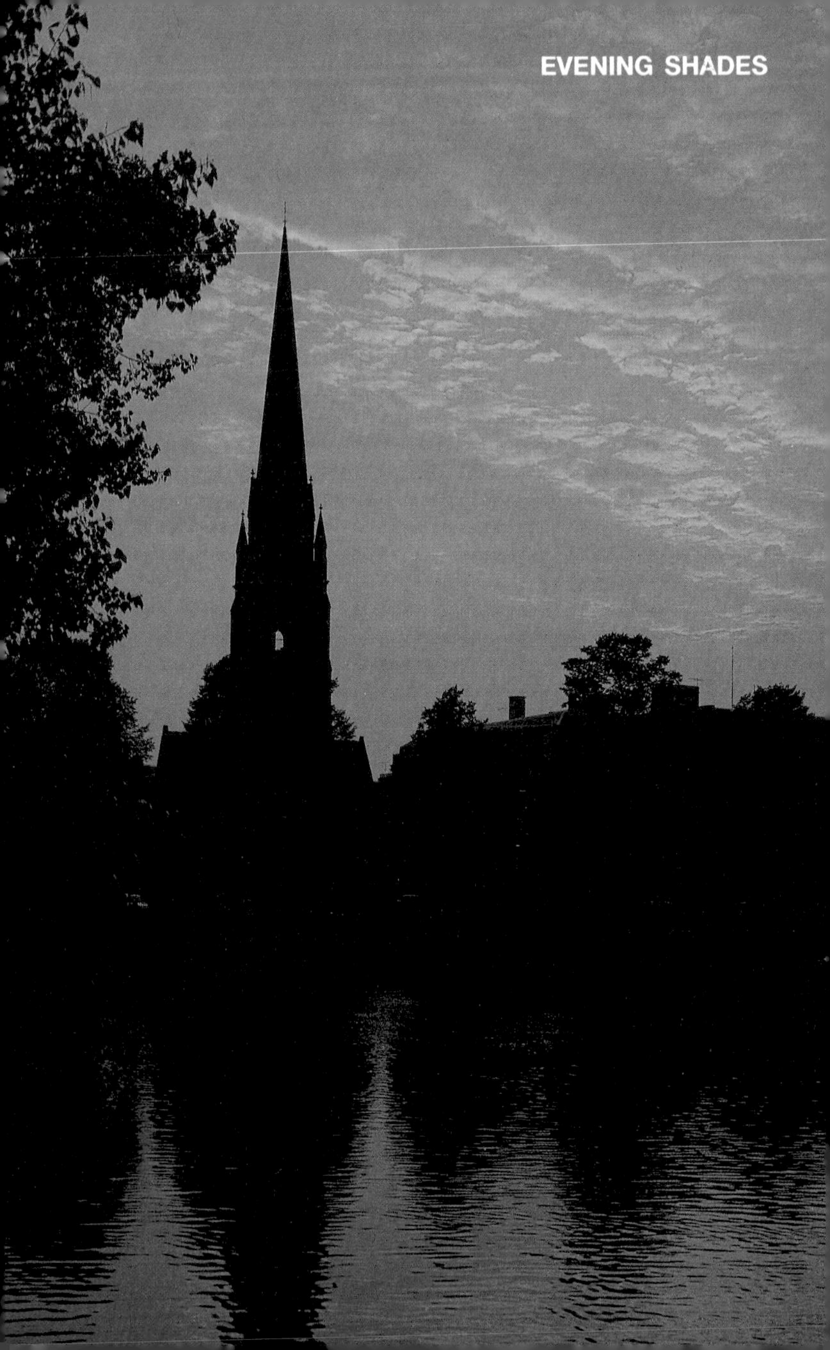
EVENING SHADES

# THE FRIENDSHIP BOOK

SATURDAY—APRIL 26.

HOW final our word good-bye sounds! The French say au revoir — "until we see each other again" which certainly has a more encouraging ring to it. The Australians say much the same, yet in their own unique style: "See you later."

I recently read about a British speaker visiting Australia, and giving a talk. He shook hands with many people afterwards as they left, and all said in a friendly way, "See you later!" The poor man began seriously to wonder if he'd been booked for another meeting which no-one had told him about!

Perhaps our own final-sounding good-bye wouldn't sound so cold and final if we remembered its original wording — "God be with ye." It is good to keep this in mind, even better if we could mean exactly that as we say our "good-byes".

SUNDAY—APRIL 27.

THE grace of our Lord Jesus Christ be with you.

Corinthians I 16:23

MONDAY—APRIL 28.

TO know someone here or there with whom you feel there is understanding in spite of distances or thoughts unexpressed — that can make of this earth a garden.

Johann Wolfgang Von Goethe.

# THE FRIENDSHIP BOOK

TUESDAY—APRIL 29.

I HAD a plumber call one time and because tools of any kind fascinate me, I had a good peek in his box. It's amazing how many different kinds there were, hidden in its depths.

Now, isn't that just like *us*; we all come into the world equipped with the tools that make up our characters, unique to us alone. It is these we have to use to work out our individual lives, and no one has exactly the same box of tools.

The plumber left, patting the pipe joint he'd just mended, and saying, "There, that's a good job done," and it was. He'd used his individual mechanical and personal tools the right way.

WEDNESDAY—APRIL 30.

FEELING a little downhearted today? Things not going too well? Perhaps, like a shopkeeper, it's time for taking stock. You may be surprised at how much you find.

*FRIENDS: Greater in number this year, and all well worth keeping.*

*NEIGHBOURS: A large selection, and many who smile and stop to chat.*

*MEMORIES: Too many to count, but stored in special containers.*

*LOVE: Vast amounts, given and received. Indestructible. Everlasting.*

Feeling better now? I do hope so. A little stocktaking works wonders.

# May

IF you are a plant lover, have you noticed when you are transplanting seedlings from one pot to another that, if you choose the next-sized pot, the plant seems to thrive better than if you use a *much* larger one?

The choice of the smaller pot seems to help the roots of the plant to reach out to the sides, encouraging growth.

We often jump into a situation in life that is too big for us to cope with, and we feel completely overwhelmed. If we begin in a modest way within our limitations, we are more likely to succeed.

From acorns sturdy oak trees will grow.

FRIDAY—MAY 2.

GOING into my favourite second-hand bookshop the other day, I came across a book of humorous quotations and one in particular caught my eye and made me smile:-

"Your Friend is the person who knows all about you, and still likes you."

This is the kind of Friend who will stand by you in times of trouble — a real Friend indeed.

PEACEFUL
PASTURES

# THE FRIENDSHIP BOOK

### SATURDAY—MAY 3.

I CAME across these lines recently, and I felt they were well worth passing on.

*What we need:*
*More doers, fewer talkers*
*More to inspire others with confidence*
*Fewer to throw cold water on any initiative*
*More to point out what's right with the world*
*Fewer to keep harping on what's wrong*
*More to be interested in lighting candles*
*Fewer in blowing them out.*

It was written with churches in mind, but don't you think it is something we could apply to every area of our life?

### SUNDAY—MAY 4.

WHETHER therefore ye eat, or drink, or whatsoever ye do, do all to the glory of God.

Corinthians I 10:31

### MONDAY—MAY 5.

WATCHING a television documentary programme on work in a children's hospital, one of the specialists said, "In any critical illness, or injury, the child who has been taught to obey has a four times better chance of recovery than the undisciplined child."

An unexpected bonus for good behaviour!

# THE FRIENDSHIP BOOK

## TUESDAY—MAY 6.

ONE of the little tasks which the Lady of the House and I look forward to carrying out each year is taking a bag or two of the bluebells which have multiplied in our garden, and planting them in the spinney at the bottom of the road. Year by year they increase there, creating a lovely carpet of blue in the early Summer.

However, two years ago we noticed that the local authority had been dredging the pond and had left ugly banks of hard sludge along the edge. We wondered if our little bulbs would be able to survive in such unpromising conditions, but we completed our planting and hoped for the best.

Last year when we returned to the woods to see what was happening, we were delighted to find that the bluebells had indeed survived and were growing well, ready to charm us.

It's a comfort to know that the circumstances of life, no matter how ugly or unpromising they appear to be at first, can sometimes with care, patience and a spirit of hope, be transformed.

## WEDNESDAY—MAY 7.

IT was an old seaman who once said to me that luck is like the tide. Sometimes, he said, it seems so far away that you think it will never come back.

That's when you have to stand firm on the beach. Walk away and you'll miss it. Stay where you are and suddenly, when you least expect it, it's back, swirling at your feet . . .

# THE FRIENDSHIP BOOK

YOU just can't please everyone all of the time. If you try, you end up by pleasing no-one, not even yourself! So, be yourself, with just a touch of the Mrs Doasyouwouldbedoneby mixed in to keep the balance right. Here's a little verse which sums it up so neatly: —

*Do what you can, be what you are;*
*Shine like a glow-worm, if you can't be a star;*
*Work like a pulley, if you can't be a crane;*
*Be a wheel-greaser, if you can't drive the train.*

"I NEVER sit down at night," Jane Welsh Carlyle wrote, "beside a good fire, alone, without feeling a need of talking a little on paper . . ."

Jane, born in Haddington, was the wife of that famous man of letters, Thomas Carlyle. She loved to write, and sent hundreds of lively letters to her friends, a selection of which have been published.

I am sure that Jane would have agreed with Anthony Trollope, the 19th-century novelist, when he wrote: "A pleasant letter I hold to be the pleasantest thing that this world has to give."

It is lovely to talk on the telephone to family and friends, but if we don't take up our pen, and "talk a little on paper" to our friends as Jane did, then we are unlikely to receive a pleasant reply beginning: "Thank you for your letter. It was so nice to hear from you . . ."

# THE FRIENDSHIP BOOK

**E**ACH year in May the Lady of the House and I make a point of having a drive to a park noted for its fine display of rhododendrons. On one visit, though, we were too early, for the buds were tightly closed and we came away disappointed. Our second visit proved disappointing as well, for there had been some overnight frosts and chilly mornings which had delayed the flowering process.

However, our third attempt was successful and we were rewarded with a wonderful show of gorgeous rhododendrons — white, cream, apricot, pink, mauve, purple, scarlet and crimson — and we sat amongst them, enjoying our picnic and revelling in the sheer beauty.

As the Lady of the House leaned back contentedly, she remarked, "Francis, doesn't this just prove the wisdom of that old proverb, 'If at first you don't succeed, try, try, try again'?"

I couldn't agree more.

**P**RESERVE me, O God: for in thee do I put my trust.

Psalm 16:1

**A** FRIEND should bear his friend's infirmities.

William Shakespeare.

**TIME FOR REFLECTION**

# THE FRIENDSHIP BOOK

THE Lady of the House and I had been on a bus journey and were returning home. Suddenly, around a bend, the bus stopped and we all looked out thinking there had been an accident.

However, standing on the road was a young and frightened cow. She had discovered an open gate and the others in the field were about to follow her.

Our driver climbed down from his cab and gently guided her back to the safety of the field, carefully fastening the gate. Other vehicles were speeding past, seemingly unaware of the hazard.

We continued our journey and I reflected how Good Samaritans appear in many disguises. Some wear overalls and drive pick-up trucks. Others travel in ambulances or police cars, while our own Samaritan wore a bus driver's uniform!

God bless all Good Samaritans — whoever they are and wherever they may be.

BILL, an old friend of mine, retired recently from a job which for the past 40 years had demanded early rising. Knowing how much he had always disliked getting up so early, I asked him if he now intended to throw away his hated alarm clock.

"Certainly not," he replied with a grin. "All my life I've had to do what that clock told me. Now that I'm my own master, I intend to keep it going for the sheer pleasure of ignoring it!"

# THE FRIENDSHIP BOOK

## THURSDAY—MAY 15.

LIFE was never easy, and most of us have a good grumble at times. I know I do, then I feel a little ashamed when I remember the words of Florence Nightingale, the nursing heroine of the Crimean War, the Lady of the Lamp of Scutari:

"Live your life while you have it, life is a splendid gift."

## FRIDAY—MAY 16.

I WAS recently told a story about John Wesley that I had not heard before.

When he wrote his sermons in that famous study room in his high old house in City Road, London, he would get carried away, and use long, difficult words. When reading them over later, he realised that few would understand them.

Knowing that his servant girls were often tired after long duties cleaning, and making meals for him and his friends, he decided to help by giving them a rest. He would sit them down and read his sermons aloud.

They enjoyed this and felt proud and honoured. If they could not understand all the text, he would alter words and phrases, using the simple ones that they suggested instead — words that everyone could understand.

Whenever he could, John Wesley always tried to work with others. Maybe this is why, even today all over the world, many still benefit from his creativity and thoughtfulness all those years ago.

# THE FRIENDSHIP BOOK

## COLOUR

*B*RIGHT, *silver pools across the lane,*
*A legacy from early rain.*
*A sky both washed and brushed, and blue*
*On this glad morning, clean and new.*
*Red boats at anchor calmly ride*
*Upon the cool, incoming tide.*
*While distant hills roll gently down*
*From purple height to woodland brown.*
*And I rejoice with heart and mind*
*In all the colour I can find.*

                                    Iris Hesselden.

SUNDAY—MAY 18.

I AM the vine, ye are the branches: He that abideth in me, and I in him, the same bringeth forth much fruit: for without me ye can do nothing.

                                    John 15:5

MONDAY—MAY 19.

A FRIEND of mine, talking of a mutual acquaintance, who had had more than her share of troubles, said, "She was a grand person, Francis, for she never put the burden down when the going got tough."

I couldn't help thinking what a lovely thing to say this was, and if only we all tried to live to such high standards how much better off everybody would be.

E

# THE FRIENDSHIP BOOK

HERE is one of Dr William Barclay's prayers that always helps me:

*O God, sometimes I begin to worry, especially when I sit at the end of the day and think.*

*I begin to worry about my work. Help me to know that with your help I can cope.*

*I begin to worry about money and making ends meet.*

*Help me to remember that, though money is important, there are things that money cannot buy — and these are the most precious things of all.*

*I begin to worry about my health. Help me to remember that worrying makes me worse, and that trusting makes me better.*

*I begin to worry about those I love. Help me to do everything I can for them, and then to leave them in your care.*

*Give me tonight your peace in my troubled heart, through Jesus Christ my Lord.*

RALPH EMERSON, the American essayist, lecturer, and poet, wrote:— "We take care of our health; we lay up money; we make our roof tight, and our clothing sufficient; but who provides wisely that he shall not be wanting in the best property of all — friends?"

A quotation to remember, don't you think?

F

# THE FRIENDSHIP BOOK

THURSDAY—MAY 22.

WAITING in a post office queue I couldn't help overhearing a conversation between two women ahead of me.

"Surely you remember that trick Nellie played on you, Kitty?" said one. Kitty shrugged her shoulders, and I waited, wondering what the trick was.

"Oh, you must remember!" said the first speaker.

"No!" exclaimed Kitty firmly, "I distinctly remember forgetting it!"

I never did hear about that trick — which is not surprising, because obviously Kitty had learned never to nurse a grudge.


FRIDAY—MAY 23.

I HEARD a story about the young niece of Charles Darwin, a man whose views on evolution in his "Origin Of Species" aroused bitter controversy because they conflicted with the account of creation in the Bible.

She said, "The Bible says that God created the world in seven days. Great-uncle Charles said it took rather longer, but we needn't worry because it's wonderful anyway."

How true! Sometimes people can get too confused about the whys and wherefores of God's creation. For myself, I prefer to accept the daily wonder of it all and to treat it with the gratitude and respect it deserves.

# THE FRIENDSHIP BOOK

THE Lady of the House had been visiting our friend Phyllis.

"How is our friend today?" I asked later. "Happy as usual, I suppose."

"Of course, and today she has given me a formula which disposes of worry for good!"

Intrigued, I asked to share the secret and I could not fault Phyllis' cure, which goes like this:

"You have only two things to worry about; you are either rich or poor. If you are rich, then you have nothing to worry about. If you are poor, however, you have two things to worry about; you are either in good health or bad health. If you are well you have nothing to worry about. If you are not well, you have two things to worry about; you will either get better or get worse.

"If you are going to get better, you have nothing to worry about. If you're not going to get better, you have two things to worry about; you are either going to Heaven or the other place. If you are going to Heaven, you have nothing to worry about. If you go to the other place, you will be so busy greeting so many old friends you won't have time to worry!"

Irrefutable logic!

HUMBLE yourselves therefore under the mighty hand of God, that he may exalt you in due time: Casting all your care upon him; for he careth for you.

Peter I 5:6-7

# THE FRIENDSHIP BOOK

<u>MONDAY—MAY 26.</u>

**P**RAYER enlarges the heart until it is capable of containing God's gift of Himself. Ask and seek, and your heart will grow big enough to receive Him and keep Him as your own.

Mother Teresa of Calcutta.

<u>TUESDAY—MAY 27.</u>

**D**URING May, June and July people in many areas are busy preparing for their local Best Kept Village competition. Gardeners can be seen putting out bedding plants, hoeing borders and keeping lawns immaculate, while others do their bit by picking up litter, sweeping footpaths and generally seeing that everything is tidy.

As it was said in one area: "It must be emphasised that the judges are looking for the best *kept* village, not the *prettiest*." The point of the competition is to encourage people to make the best of what they have. Absence of litter, care of open spaces, playing fields and public places, good notice-boards with up-to-date information have nothing to do with the prettiness of a village — but everything to do with a proper sense of pride in our surroundings.

As in so many things, the importance is not solely in working for the honour of winning, but in the real satisfaction and benefit to all that comes through teamwork, co-operation and a good community spirit.

DEEP
IN THOUGHT

# THE FRIENDSHIP BOOK

IN my young days, there was always one youth hostel which was a particular delight — it was quiet and far from habitation.

Situated at Garsdale in Yorkshire, it had once been a farmhouse owned by Robert Macfie, a Scottish sugar merchant. The approach was impressive and interesting — you went through a large gate, down a tree-lined lane to Place Farm where the farmer would chat about the Dales.

Then came a steep climb to the house — what a pull it was — but how lovely at the top, and what a view.

We slept in a dormitory that had once been filled with Mr Macfie's treasures which included grand pianos, violins and his library. How did he get them there in the days before tractors? It must have been a struggle, I thought, before dropping off to sleep.

I now know that life is like this, too. Anything worth having, often means a struggle and facing up to obstacles along the way — but what a reward we receive when we reach our goal!

HERE is something for us to think about today as we go about living our lives:

"Nothing is worth more than this day."

Those thoughtful words were written by the great German writer Goethe.

# THE FRIENDSHIP BOOK

FRIDAY—MAY 30.

"**D**ADDY, what's that?" said the little boy, looking up at the plaque on the wall above his pew.

"That's in memory of all the brave men who died in the services."

Awestruck, the little boy scanned the long list of names, then said, "I see, Daddy, but were they the morning or evening services?"


SATURDAY—MAY 31.

**M**Y friend Bill, an experienced gardener, called round while I was putting in my broad bean plants.

"They look good and healthy, Francis," he said, "but don't you think you have planted the rows too far apart?"

I was surprised and explained that because the plants grew so large, I needed room to get between the rows when the beans were ready for picking.

"You're quite right," said Bill, "but broad beans get knocked over easily, so they need the support of another row close by. If you plant two rows close together with a wide space between them and the next rows, the plants will support each other, and you'll still have plenty of room for picking the beans."

So often the lessons of nature can be of help in life. If a crisis comes along and we have the support of loved ones, it enables us to stand upright and keep on our feet — just like the broad beans.

# June

SUNDAY—JUNE 1.

AND he said, The Lord is my rock, and my fortress, and my deliverer. The God of my rock; in him will I trust, he is my shield, and the horn of my salvation, my high tower, and my refuge, my saviour; thou savest me from violence.

Samuel II 22:2-3

MONDAY—JUNE 2.

I WAS in our newsagent's choosing magazines for the Lady of the House, who was a little under the weather, when the shop assistant came through a door in a burst of song. When she spotted me, she flushed with embarrassment.

"I'm sorry," she said, "I didn't think anyone was there."

"That's all right, Christine," I replied. "I enjoyed your song. You sound very happy today."

"Oh, I am," she said. "I love working here!"

How nice it was for me, too, to start the day with such a cheerful encounter. In the words of Ecclesiasticus: "The gladness of the heart is the life of man, and the joyfulness of a man prolongeth his days."

That's the spirit!

# THE FRIENDSHIP BOOK

SIR CHRISTOPHER WREN, the great architect, asked three men who were building St Paul's Cathedral what they were doing.

One said, "I'm labouring here until knocking off time." Another said, "I'm working for money." The third replied, "I'm helping Sir Christopher Wren to build this cathedral."

I reckon that third man had discovered the great secret of a positive attitude to work — a pride in what he was doing. Yes, I know work can be irksome at times, the same thing over and over again maybe, like doing the washing-up! But adopting the third man's attitude will surely keep us from wearying.

GEORGE had put together an unusual ornament in the garden . . . a lion's head spouting water into a small trough filled with stones.

The sound was very pleasant as the water trickled over the smooth stones, but George wasn't happy with the effect until he found a stone with a pitted surface. He placed it directly under the spout and, as the water hit the irregular stone, it made a much more interesting sound.

How often this is true of people, too. The ones who are full of character and interest are those whose lives have been textured by experiencing the rough as well as the smooth.

# THE FRIENDSHIP BOOK

<u>THURSDAY—JUNE 5.</u>

"THERE'S only bad news in the papers," moaned a friend recently.

I started to cut out the good news from each issue of our paper. A week had almost passed when I noticed the pile was growing steadily each day.

It consisted of a short item about the bravery of a pet dog; the gallantry of a man who tried to deter car thieves and succeeded. Then there was the news report of a couple, and their happy photograph, who had just celebrated 65 years of marriage, and details of a child successfully recovering from a heart operation.

No good news? There is plenty if you look for it.

<u>FRIDAY—JUNE 6.</u>

THE school inspector got a surprise when he asked the scripture class if anyone could tell him who had knocked down the Walls of Jericho. A girl in the front row put up her hand and said, "Please sir, it wasn't me."

Turning to the teacher, the inspector said, "What do you think of this answer?"

"Well," came the reply, "I have always found her to be truthful and if she says she didn't do it, I believe her."

Quite nonplussed, the inspector went to the headmaster's room to relate what had happened.

"I'm sorry," said the headmaster, taking out a cheque book. "How much do you think they'll cost to repair?"

A true tale? I hope not!

# THE FRIENDSHIP BOOK

SATURDAY—JUNE 7.

CHARLES KINGSLEY, author of those well-loved classics "Westward Ho!" and "The Water-Babies", said:—

"The men whom I have seen succeed best in life have always been cheerful and hopeful men, who went about their business with a smile on their faces, and took the changes and chances of this mortal life like men, facing rough and smooth alike as it came."

Words to remember as we each proceed through *our* life, don't you think?

SUNDAY—JUNE 8.

NOW faith is the substance of things hoped for, the evidence of things not seen.

Hebrews 11:1

MONDAY—JUNE 9.

THE Lady of the House often goes round the many gardens which are open to the public at this time of year, and really enjoys the beauty created there.

It reminded me of the lovely words written by Maurice Maeterlinck:

"Where would we be if humanity had not known flowers? If they didn't exist or had always been hidden from our sight . . . would our character, our morals, our aptitude for beauty, our happiness be the same?"

# THE FRIENDSHIP BOOK

<u>TUESDAY—JUNE 10.</u>

A FRIEND accompanied his small nephew to buy his birthday present for his mother; an important affair, and one which had to be kept secret. However, he was so excited that on returning home, he ran into the house shouting:

"Mummy, Mummy, where can I hide this so you won't find it?"

<u>WEDNESDAY—JUNE 11.</u>

B ARBARA and Keith often go to Spain for their holidays. As they both speak Spanish fluently, they are able to enjoy everything that the country has to offer throughout the many and varied regions they have visited.

I am telling you this — and I know they won't mind — because in the past they both failed Spanish examinations. When they were at school, they seemed to have great difficulty mastering the ins and outs of the language. However, by sheer perseverance they passed the dreaded exams in adulthood, and now communicate readily in Spanish. Incidentally, studying at evening classes brought them together in the first place, and they are now man and wife!

The point of all this? Surely it is worth reminding ourselves that achievements rarely come easily. If you are sometimes discouraged with your efforts, remember the story of Barbara and Keith. Just try, try again!

JUST A
BACK GARDEN

# THE FRIENDSHIP BOOK

<u>THURSDAY—JUNE 12.</u>

A T our library I found a fascinating little book. It answered obscure questions that we've all wondered about, but have never been able to answer.

I was intrigued by one answer. It was about golf balls and why they have dimples. Evidently the dimples make the balls travel a great deal farther than a smooth ball.

This reminded me of the dimples that appear on our faces when we smile. These dimples are very precious, too, and should be cultivated. At the right time and in the right place they can help happiness to spread. So, try to greet both the stress and serenity of life with a smile and a dimple — they will carry farther.

<u>FRIDAY—JUNE 13.</u>

"T HE postman brought me another letter from my friend, Amy," said Helen happily. That sounds at first like a very ordinary statement and nothing to get excited about, but when I tell you that my friend Helen, is 84 and has been exchanging letters, and later phone calls, with Amy since they were schoolgirls together, then you'll realise what a special friendship it is.

"Yes, it *is* special," agreed my elderly friend when I remarked on it. "You see, when Amy had to move away with her parents, we were both devastated, and agreed we must keep in touch."

"Indeed you have, all these years," I marvelled.

"Of course," she said simply, "we promised, you see."

# THE FRIENDSHIP BOOK

## SATURDAY—JUNE 14.

AN old friend once said to me, "You know, Francis, to be able to shut your own front door behind you is a great thing."

I knew that she meant to have the independence of your own home is a pearl without price, and so it is. Perhaps, too, at certain times in our lives we see our closed front door as shutting out a less than sympathetic world. However, to be able to open wide our own front door to welcome in our friends is also a great thing — and have you ever thought that our open front doors are gateways for ourselves into a wonderfully interesting world?

## SUNDAY—JUNE 15.

WHOSOEVER heareth these sayings of mine, and doeth them, I will liken him unto a wise man, which built his house upon a rock.

Matthew 7:24

## MONDAY—JUNE 16.

WHILE I was in Southampton recently, I was intrigued to see three or four little tug boats fussing around a huge liner and was told that the huge ship would be unable to turn without the help of these little boats.

Don't we all, however grand and clever we are, need the help of others, even though they may seem self-effacing, to help us through the waters of life?

# THE FRIENDSHIP BOOK

<u>TUESDAY—JUNE 17.</u>

CHARLES is a very old and close friend. We met years ago at the rambling club and have a great deal in common.

At the end of the day after one of our long walks together, we sometimes realise that we have hardly said a word to each other. We have simply enjoyed each other's company and, without speaking, somehow always know what each other is thinking.

We have learned that friendship does not always need conversation — it has its very own language of communication.

<u>WEDNESDAY—JUNE 18.</u>

WHEN I was on holiday in Belgium, I went into a café for a coffee. It was obviously a popular place, for the only vacant seat was beside an elderly man.

I smiled and shrugged as I took the chair, he smiled and nodded back to me, then to my dismay — for my French is minimal — began chatting away. Trying to save embarrassment, I used sign language to try to indicate that his language was not mine, but still he went on talking.

Then suddenly I realised he just needed someone to talk to. So I took my cue from his expressions, and smiled when he smiled, laughed when he did, appeared solemn when it seemed apt. Finally I had to leave him, a smiling "au revoir" was all that was needed, and we parted like old friends.

Yes indeed, companionship, like music, is international, and so is the "listening ear".

F

# THE FRIENDSHIP BOOK

<u>THURSDAY—JUNE 19.</u>

"IF you think too far ahead you miss the shot," I often hear Wimbledon champions say when I watch the annual tennis tournament on television. To them it is a cardinal rule of the game. It is impossible for them to plan their strategy too far ahead, and win.

Isn't that a rule for life, too? Sometimes an unexpected event completely changes our work and life. We cannot tell what the future will hold.

Instead of taking life steadily to achieve our goal, we often hurry and worry, becoming nervous because things aren't working out as quickly as we had planned and in the end we "miss the shot".

We are often advised to live a day at a time, and if we can do this, it helps.

<u>FRIDAY—JUNE 20.</u>

THESE days we see so many advertisements telling us — both men and women — how to have beautiful hands and a smooth skin without wrinkles, even when we reach old age.

If all these suggestions worked for us, it would be difficult to choose the correct one. It is very commendable to be clean, to look neat, to feel happy and to present ourselves as best we can, whatever our age. Here is a thought from Charles Dickens on the subject — it really works and doesn't cost a penny. He said: "Cheerfulness and content are great beautifiers and preservers of youthful looks."

So try it — starting today!

# THE FRIENDSHIP BOOK

<u>SATURDAY—JUNE 21.</u>

OUR friend Ken had a stroke some time ago, a severe one which for a time left him without speech and movement. Thankfully he has made an excellent recovery and is now able to look after himself, and with the help of his stick is confident enough to set off by bus to visit different places.

He was telling us about the help and kindness he has received now that he has joined the ranks of the disabled, particularly from bus drivers.

"They have to wait quite a time while I clamber on board," he said, "but they never show the slightest impatience. There's always a cheerful smile for me, and they never set off until I am safely in my seat. They needn't do it, but they do. So," he went on, "I wrote to the bus manager to say thank you. After all, what's the use of feeling grateful if I don't express it?"

How true! If only more of us remembered to express our thanks, what a happier place the world would be.

<u>SUNDAY—JUNE 22.</u>

THY word is a lamp unto my feet, and a light unto my path.

Psalm 119:105

<u>MONDAY—JUNE 23.</u>

THERE is nothing mightier and nobler than when man and wife are of one heart and mind.

Homer.

# THE FRIENDSHIP BOOK

TO my mind there is nothing more evocative of a Summer's day than a daisy-spangled lawn or meadow. Medicinally the juice of the daisy leaves was used in medieval times as a remedy for gout and rheumatism, and it was believed that if heated and inhaled it would cure migraine.

Officially Spring is said to commence on 21st March, but an old country saying proclaimed that Spring had arrived when you could put a foot on three daisies.

With the coming of Midsummer's Day on 24th June, village girls used to gather in the meadows and with eyes closed, pick a handful of grass. There was great excitement as they examined their bunch, for the number of daisies in it, they believed, indicated the number of years they would have to wait until their wedding day!

So this small white flower will always have a special place in *my* heart, for the lovely qualities it symbolises — innocence and fidelity.

AS we were driving along at the time of the Wimbledon tennis season and passed a little church, the Lady of the House saw a sign on the notice-board: "Love Won Another."

We felt it was a lovely Christian message. By loving and caring for others we are helping other people to the love of Christ.

SOFT AND
GLOW

# THE FRIENDSHIP BOOK

<u>THURSDAY—JUNE 26.</u>

**H**ERE'S a short verse I've found about words. I don't know who wrote it, but it expresses all that I'd ever need to say:

### A WORD
*A careless word may kindle strife,*
*A cruel word may wreck a life,*
*A bitter word may hate instil,*
*A brutal word may smite and kill.*
*A gracious word may light a day,*
*A kindly word may keep loneliness away,*
*A timely word may lessen stress,*
*A loving word may heal and bless.*

It's always as well to stop to think before we speak or write.

<u>FRIDAY—JUNE 27.</u>

**I**T was nice to come across this story about the late Duchess of Kent, Princess Marina. She liked to go for walks, hoping to remain unrecognised.

One day, in Hyde Park, she was alarmed to see two American tourists bearing down upon her — intent, she thought, on taking her photograph. However, to her surprise and delight she found they were looking for someone to take a picture of themselves together.

The Duchess willingly obliged. So somewhere in America there is probably a shot of two smiling Americans, and neither of them, nor the friends who have seen it, have the slightest idea that it is the work of a royal photographer.

# THE FRIENDSHIP BOOK

O N 29th June 1927 there occurred that rare event — a total eclipse of the sun — visible in the North of England. It stirred the imagination of a young Yorkshire lad who wrote notes about what he had seen. His father encouraged him.

"Write something every day and you'll get a nice diary at Christmas," he said. The boy did so, got his diary for 1928 and continued to make his jottings.

This boy was none other than William Foggitt of Thirsk, whose predictions about the weather, based on observations of the behaviour of birds, animals, and plants earned him fame. Bill Foggitt won a nationwide reputation as a weather prophet whose predictions reached the national press.

How wise it was of Father Foggitt to encourage his son all those years ago. How many countrymen have benefited from the skills young William eventually developed!

S EARCH the scriptures; for in them ye think ye have eternal life: and they are they which testify of me.

John 5:39

I DON'T want to undermine your confidence, but if you feel you are sitting on top of the world, just remember it turns over every 24 hours.

Be ready!

# July

I ALWAYS take a book on holiday with me. One weekend the Lady of the House and I decided to spend a few days at a cottage in Yorkshire. On arrival I unpacked and found that my gardening book was missing — I'd left it at home.

Fortunately, there was a bookcase in the cottage and there I found one of W. Riley's novels. It was not quite the reading I'd intended, but I found these words: "Happiness is a plant that will grow in any soil that is watered by love and service but withers in the hot sun of selfishness."

When I came across this, I was pleased that I had forgotten my own book because it provided such food for thought. So each day now let's try to water our own soil with love and service and, sure enough, we'll surely find that happiness *does* grow and flourish!

WEDNESDAY—JULY 2.

A CHILD's soul is like a bank; what you put in, you get back, ten years hence, with interest.

Father Borelli of Naples.

# THE FRIENDSHIP BOOK

<u>THURSDAY—JULY 3.</u>

BILL JONES went through a bad time. I won't go into details, but he took on too much, his health suffered, and he had a nervous breakdown.

So I was amazed to see how well he is looking now when I met him in the street. "Yes, I feel great, Francis," he said with a grin. "In fact, I've never felt better. I have reorganised my life and I'm really enjoying myself. You could say," he added with a twinkle, "that I have turned a breakdown into a breakthrough!"

Well done, Bill, and well done, all those who fight back against adversity, and win.

<u>FRIDAY—JULY 4.</u>

WE consider ourselves fortunate because an old friend, George, lives near the magnificent Royal Horticultural Society's garden at Wisley in Surrey. Every year, we are able to combine a visit to both George and the showpiece gardens.

On one such visit, George said, "You know, when I am feeling low, I don my walking shoes and come here, and I guarantee it isn't long before I'm feeling very much better. There is so much here to cheer me — beautiful species to catch the eye; clever grafting of one tree to another; magnificent displays of colourful, tropical plants in the glasshouses; tiny alpines, and so much more."

Later, when back in my own home, I thought of the privilege those gardeners have, to create such a place of beauty, peace and cheer for the many thousands of visitors. Long may they continue!

G

# THE FRIENDSHIP BOOK

SATURDAY—JULY 5.

WHEN William Booth was engaged in his early campaign work in England he called his movement The Christian Mission. Then, one day, he was standing by one of his assistants, a man called Railton, who was writing a letter.

Booth saw him pen the words: "The Christian Mission is a volunteer army."

On impulse, Booth lent over, took the pen and stroked out the word "volunteer". In its place he wrote "salvation".

Thus, in an instant, the Salvation Army was born. We take the name for granted, but that moment's inspiration is worth recording and remembering as crucial in the founding of a great and well-loved movement.


SUNDAY—JULY 6.

EVERY man according as he purposeth in his heart, so let him give; not grudgingly, or of necessity: for God loveth a cheerful giver.

Corinthians II 9:7


MONDAY—JULY 7.

I FOUND this little tit-bit in an old copy of the parish magazine of Little Bowden Church in Leicestershire:—

A reporter once asked Mahatma Gandhi what he thought of Western civilisation. His reply was, "I think it would be a very good idea."

H

# THE FRIENDSHIP BOOK

<u>TUESDAY—JULY 8.</u>

ARE you feeling good? Pleased that you have done all that you could to help those around you? No guilty feelings at all?

Then just pause and think of the old proverb which tells us that all too often a clear conscience is simply the result of a bad memory!

<u>WEDNESDAY—JULY 9.</u>

TWO men were sitting on a river bank enjoying the beauty and the silence. Said the first one, "What a perfect river to sit by with a good book." His friend replied, "Who needs a book?"

It put me in mind of Isaac Walton when he extolled the merits of his own peaceful situation. "No life so happy and so pleasant as the life of a well-governed angler," he wrote, "for when the lawyer is swallowed up with business, and the statesman is preventing or contriving plots, then we sit on cowslip banks, hear the birds sing and possess ourselves in as much quietness as these silent silver streams, which we now see glide so quietly by us."

The poet Gerard Manley Hopkins expressed his own feelings about the beauty of nature when he wrote: "Look at the stars! Look, look up at the skies," while Wordsworth exclaimed: "My heart leaps up when I behold a rainbow in the sky."

So, on this lovely, Summer's day, I, too, will take time to be grateful for all the wonders of nature that, in an often busy world, relax my body and fill my heart with peace. Will you join me?

# THE FRIENDSHIP BOOK

<u>THURSDAY—JULY 10.</u>

WHEN I have the chance, I like to watch sports programmes on television. I particularly like cricket and tennis in Summer and football and rugby in Winter.

What strikes me about some of the players who excel and have reached the top of their profession, is their humility about it all. It can't be easy to be humble, especially when they are so far ahead in terms of ability and win matches time and again all over the world.

One athlete I heard being interviewed made a remark that I will always remember. He said that his parents and his trainer had taught him from an early age that if he did not learn humility, he would at some stage learn humiliation.

This is worth thinking about, isn't it?

<u>FRIDAY—JULY 11.</u>

WHEN our young friends Paul and Daniel spent a week's holiday on a farm, they were unable to get to sleep one evening until quite late because of the excitement of looking out their bedroom window to watch the hay being baled.

For many of the older generation it may not be so easy to see things through the eyes of a child and recapture the wonder again. However, what a lot we miss when we take things for granted.

When, I wonder, did we last gaze in awe at the sight of a rosebud, a fragile spider's web or a glorious sunset?

# THE FRIENDSHIP BOOK

SATURDAY—JULY 12.

"I HAVE known many troubles. Most of them have never happened," said the American author Mark Twain.

Yet on reading his biography, you realise he had faced many difficulties and overcome them. His words, however, are a good reminder that sometimes worries are not necessary. One remedy for facing those that do exist is the old one of living a day at a time.

SUNDAY—JULY 13.

AND Naomi said unto her daughter in law, Blessed be he of the Lord, who hath not left off his kindness to the living and to the dead.

Ruth 2:20

MONDAY—JULY 14.

HAVE you ever noticed that after a hot sunny spell of weather someone is sure to say, "But the gardens need rain!" Then, after a spell of rain for several days, the same folk will say, "Oh, the garden needs sunshine."

I was talking about this to an old gardener friend of mine and asked him what his philosophy was.

"Oh," he replied, "I leave it to Him up above. After all, He made the flowers and plants, so He must know what they want and I reckon He gives them just that."

If only we could all be as tolerant of the weather, no matter what it is!

A PATH
TO FOLLOW

# THE FRIENDSHIP BOOK

<u>TUESDAY—JULY 15.</u>

I WENT to see Old Henry in his new house. He used to live on a very quiet road, but now he's on a busy street and, as we sat chatting, the traffic was rumbling by. "Don't you mind it?" I asked.

"I love it!" he exclaimed. "I like to watch the lorries and see where they've come from. Then there are the buses . . . They're from all over the country — often places I knew when I was young. What memories they bring back!"

Henry is more or less confined to the house now, but he'll never be a prisoner. His mind roves as freely as ever. I left him eagerly scanning the flow of traffic, loving every minute of it.


<u>WEDNESDAY—JULY 16.</u>

I HAVE to attend several committee meetings during the year. We each want to make our point, and in spite of being kept in order by our chairman, our voices gradually grow louder and louder. I sometimes sit back and think of the proverb: "Empty vessels make the most noise!"

My friend Gillian can teach us a lesson on this subject. She is a quiet soul and never shouts to make her point. She is also very musical and adjudicates at music festivals throughout the country, always going about her duties with quietness and confidence.

Gillian is well respected, not because she raises her voice to get her own way, but because hers is the way of quietness and patience.

# THE FRIENDSHIP BOOK

THURSDAY—JULY 17.

WE always look forward to Thursday evenings because that's when our cheerful vegetable man comes. He is well over 70, but calls each week, delivering fruit, vegetables and other groceries.

He never fails, whatever the weather, and what is perhaps more important — he is always in a good mood and ready with a joke and a smile. Thursdays just wouldn't be the same without him!

FRIDAY—JULY 18.

THOSE of us who love Yorkshire know that Summer in the high Pennines can often be cool, rainy and overcast.

One July as the Lady of the House and I were travelling on the Settle to Carlisle railway watching the clouds and sunshine making a delightful picture on the lovely hillsides in between the showers, I suddenly thought of a story I once read about a boy who lived in the Dales.

His teacher was giving him an art lesson — showing him how to paint some large white clouds. He thought for a moment and then said, "Miss, where I live the clouds are mucky, not white!"

The weather in our country can always teach us a lesson about life. It can rain, be chilly and windy all year round, yet a rainbow, fleecy clouds and sunshine usually come after the bad spells.

Yes, the clouds in life, too, don't last for ever — they aren't always "mucky", either!

## SATURDAY—JULY 19.

A S teenagers, some of us had film or pop stars as our idols, and we believed them to be happier than we were because of all the fun that they seemed to have — glamorous parties, expensive cars, luxurious homes and holidays. However, so many of their memoirs have shown us that this was not so; having fun did not bring lasting happiness.

To achieve this we must not cling to the belief that a fun-filled, pain-free life will bring a blissful existence — more often than not, things that lead to happiness involve some pain. Working with and for those not so fortunate as ourselves; doing some charitable work; studying hard and passing exams; parenthood; the giving of ourselves, not taking all we can get, are maybe just a few.

When we realise this, our lives are changed because we know we have found the path to true happiness.

## SUNDAY—JULY 20.

T HE Lord is my light and my salvation; whom shall I fear? the Lord is the strength of my life, of whom shall I be afraid?

Psalms 27:1

## MONDAY—JULY 21.

W HEN Christ came into my life, I came about like a well-handled ship.

Robert Louis Stevenson.

# THE FRIENDSHIP BOOK

MANY of the things written in my old autograph album raise a smile when I read them again. A few hold a more serious message, such as this verse a friend wrote many years ago:—

*Your future lies before you*
*Like a bed of purest snow;*
*Be careful how you tread it,*
*For every step will show.*

I LISTEN to many radio and television programmes about gardening. I try to understand how to deal with weeds and all sorts of gardening pests, but whatever I do they persist. However, like other gardeners, I carry on undeterred.

Each month I try to do as the professional gardeners advise. In spite of weeds, slugs, bad weather and the like, I concentrate on the beauty and fulfilment of my patch.

Have you noticed how many gardeners carry this underlying sense of optimism into their daily living? They have faith and hope, and seem to know that there is still plenty of brightness ahead.

Gardeners are often loving and caring people, too. Flowers, fruit and vegetables are given away with great generosity to brighten the lives of others who have no garden or allotment.

Yes, many keen gardeners over the years have taught me to have not only faith and hope, but love.

# THE FRIENDSHIP BOOK

*YOU stand at the gateway,*
*St Peter,*
*You'd like to know what I have done*
*To allow me to walk through those portals,*
*What kind of a race have I run.*

*Well, I haven't done deeds that are noble,*
*Accomplished all this or all that,*
*But if I could help friend or neighbour,*
*I'd be there at the drop of a hat.*

*I cannot claim wisdom or learning,*
*I'm a plain, simple person, you see,*
*But I'd do what I can, to help fellow man,*
*Whether or not they'd help me.*

*I'm afraid I don't merit gold medals,*
*So I can't hold my head up with pride —*
*Did I hear you correctly, St Peter?*
*Was it, "Welcome — pass friend —*
*for you've tried!"*

Dorothy M. Loughran.

A SPEAKER was addressing a group of writers. Stressing the importance of constant efforts to improve, she said: "The only place that I know where success comes before work is in the dictionary."

# THE FRIENDSHIP BOOK

SATURDAY—JULY 26.

I ONCE read a story about a holy man who gave up wealth and position and went into the forest to live a life of prayer and simplicity.

One day he was invited to go into the town to see the new church that had been built. When he reached the door he stopped and said, "I'm sorry, there's no room. I can't get in."

"But we have reserved a place for you at the front!" said the people.

He replied, "I shall never get as far as that. The building is crammed full of words and ideas and plans. Make some space to receive God, and then I'll come back and pray with you."

As I say, it is just a story. Yet, for those of us who tend to get overwhelmed with everyday affairs, it is a reminder that perhaps we need to leave room for the essential things of life.


SUNDAY—JULY 27.

COME unto me, all ye that labour and are heavy laden, and I will give you rest.

Matthew 11:28


MONDAY—JULY 28.

A BABY boy was born in a village. He weighed 11 lbs, and the news soon spread. A little girl overhearing this information hurried home to her mother to say that Mrs Watson had a baby boy, costing £11.

SWANS —
STONES —
SERENITY

# THE FRIENDSHIP BOOK

TUESDAY—JULY 29.

*IF you love your fellow man*
*You'll go that second mile,*
*But how much more it means to him*
*If you do it with a smile.*

                                    Kathleen M. Clark.

WEDNESDAY—JULY 30.

MY father used to say that a compliment was a "verbal gift". So if you say, "What, this old thing? I've had it for years!" when somebody admires something you are wearing, or if somebody remarks that your hair looks attractive and you say, "Oh, it's an awful mess. I haven't been to the hairdresser for ages", you are not only throwing their "gift" in their faces, but you are also casting doubts on their judgement.

How much nicer if you say, "Well, thank you very much. It's kind of you to say so."

After all, it's only pouring a little oil on the wheels of life — and all our "wheels" need that sometimes!

THURSDAY—JULY 31.

HERE'S an encouraging thought if things are difficult just now:—

If you're finding the going tough, that's good, because it means you must be fighting back.

# August

## FRIDAY—AUGUST 1.

I LIKE this quotation from an old autograph book:

"Friends are like stars — we see their light most clearly on the darkest night."

## SATURDAY—AUGUST 2.

WHEN the invitation to Felicity's wedding arrived through Connie's door she was very proud, for they were next-door neighbours and she had known Felicity since childhood. Yet, at the same time, she was worried. What was she to give as a wedding present, for all she had was her pension?

Then she had an idea. Each week she picked fruit from her garden — gooseberries, strawberries, raspberries and redcurrants — and made it into jam. When the pots were all neatly labelled, she knocked at Felicity's door.

"That's the nicest wedding present I've received," said Felicity, giving Connie a hug. "You've given me a *real* housewife's store cupboard." The mutual pleasure in Connie's and Felicity's eyes was lovely to behold, so I'm told.

The best gift is a gift from the heart.

# THE FRIENDSHIP BOOK

GRACE be with you, mercy, and peace, from God the Father, and from the Lord Jesus Christ, the Son of the Father, in truth and love.

John II 1:3

I DON'T know what you'll think of it, but I agree with every word of this poem which was composed by Margaret Regan of Earls Barton, Northamptonshire:

*Don't tell me dragons are now out of date,*
*Or that unicorns don't exist.*
*Don't say Santa Claus is a fairytale*
*Surrounded by mythical mist.*
*Don't tell me that clouds can't make faces*
*or shapes*
*Of castles that rise to the sun.*
*Don't say that rabbits can't talk to each other*
*When they're out on the grass having fun.*
*Don't tell me the leprechauns, fairies and such*
*No longer, in Ireland, run wild.*
*For then I will tell you, my cynical friend,*
*To look through the eyes of a child.*

THE only reward of virtue is virtue: the only way to have a friend is to be one.

Ralph Waldo Emerson.

# THE FRIENDSHIP BOOK

I CALL to mind hearing a speaker telling of a train journey she had to make, when because of hold-ups on the line, she missed her connection. There would be nearly two hours' delay, as a result.

What was she going to do? Join in the chorus of moans and groans, or find a better way to fill the time?

She chose the latter — she'd never explored the town in which they were stranded. Now she did so, and a most rewarding exploration it turned out to be — a fine old church, a riverside walk, a row of well-preserved peaceful almshouses . . . two hours packed with happy and fulfilling discoveries.

All this came about because she'd been positive.

A TELEVISION programme I always find interesting is "The Antiques Roadshow", where experts enthuse over treasures of the past.

In particular, I enjoyed seeing genial Henry Sandon talking about pots. Pots, porcelain and china have an endearing charm.

I was interested to read, in an article by Henry, that he is just as thrilled by a cheap, damaged pot; in fact, he likes to provide a "home for sick pots".

Henry looks at a pot and hears it say, "I've got to come and live with you." No wonder he has a collection of thousands!

It's comforting to know there's a Master Potter with a place for *us* — no matter how chipped, or even cracked, we become!

# THE FRIENDSHIP BOOK

LET'S reflect on the wise words of this proverb today:- "Friendships multiply joys and divide griefs."

### VOYAGE

*LIFE's an adventure*
*On which we embark,*
*A cruise on the ocean,*
*A sail in the dark.*
*At times in the shallows*
*Where waters are warm,*
*Then tossed on the high tide*
*And lashed by the storm.*
*The wind in the rigging*
*May carry us far,*
*Hold fast to your compass*
*And follow your star.*
*And then, in the twilight,*
*Weigh anchor once more,*
*Hold your course steady*
*And pull for the shore.*

Iris Hesselden.

AND we know that all things work together for good to them that love God, to them who are the called according to his purpose.

Romans 8:28

# THE FRIENDSHIP BOOK

MONDAY—AUGUST 11.

I WAS at a Flower Show recently, and one of the exhibits was a display of pot plants from our Over 60s Club. As I stood there admiring the display, a judge placed a first prize ticket against a fine healthy begonia, and I smiled happily. No, it wasn't one of my plants, but I did know the story behind that particular beauty.

It had been given to Laura by her grandson, and Laura had lavished on it all the care possible in her circumstances, for Laura is crippled with rheumatism and spends much time in one room. The begonia stood on her window-sill, and Laura not only fed and watered it carefully, but moved it during the day so that it would catch the best light and every possible ray of sunshine. She and her plant certainly deserved that prize.

TUESDAY—AUGUST 12.

WHEN it's the holiday season I sometimes find it annoying to go round to a favourite shop and see the notice:— "Closed for staff holidays". The customers of a certain baker had to smile last season, though, for his notice was decidedly witty:—

*We knead the rest*
*So raised the dough —*
*Gone to bake in the sun*
*Return August 31.*

I wonder if he spent the time "loafing" about?

# THE FRIENDSHIP BOOK

AFTER a perfect weekend as guests in a delightful country cottage, we returned home pondering on the art of being a good hostess.

The ideal expressed by the New Zealand writer Rita Snowden was: "No one crosses our door step of right without a loving welcome."

Novelist Elizabeth Goudge wrote: "When great deeds are done by men, there's always a woman in the background and generally in the kitchen."

Last but not least is the anonymous one, probably suggested tongue in cheek: "Hospitality is the art of making people feel at home, even when you wish they *were* at home."

*MOST every day the brown thrush sings,*
*The swallows fly on tiny wings,*
*The sun wakes up a rosy red,*
*To light the day that lies ahead.*

*Most days, my heart is free and light,*
*The world seems filled with sweet delight,*
*Most days, I toil and play and rest,*
*Doing the work I love the best.*

*All skies are His — both grey and blue —*
*The storms and sweetest sunshine, too,*
*And so I trust to Him my soul,*
*The world He made from Pole to Pole.*

Margaret H. Dixon.

## FRIDAY—AUGUST 15.

ONCE, at a prayer meeting, a well-known public speaker recited the 23rd Psalm. Everyone listened in awed silence as he proclaimed the words in his superb resounding voice: "The Lord is my shepherd, I shall not want . . ."

When he sat down, one of the group said, "Yes, that was admirable, and now I'm going to ask James to read the same psalm."

Spoken in his gentle, thoughtful tones, the lines took on a deeper meaning. It was a moving experience.

When he finished, the public speaker rose. "I have a confession to make," he said. "The difference between what you have just heard from James, and what you heard from me, is this: I know the Psalm, James knows the Shepherd."

## SATURDAY—AUGUST 16.

I AM feeling guilty, for I did not make a promised phone call to a friend of ours, until reminded more than once by the Lady of the House.

Don't you think it is often the accumulation of small neglects, which cause a friendship to wither away? Such things as the unwritten letter, the forgotten birthday and Christmas cards, and the appointments to meet which are casually broken.

If we wish to keep our friends, perhaps we should remember the following wise words attributed to the Greek philosopher Aristotle:

"We should behave to our friends as we would wish our friends to behave to us."

NO WORRIES

# THE FRIENDSHIP BOOK

JESUS saith unto them, My meat is to do the will of him that sent me, and to finish his work.

John 4:34

*LOVE cannot be measured, nor counted and stored,*
*It cannot be saved in some miserly hoard.*
*Love grows and increases when given away,*
*It blossoms with kindness and blooms every day.*

*It knows no divisions, no borders nor creeds,*
*But thrives among thoughtfulness, sowing fresh seeds.*
*Unseeking, unselfish and eager to share,*
*Love triumphs in trouble and shines through despair.*

*The bounty of heaven is faith, hope and truth,*
*The wisdom of age and the courage of youth.*
*So many great blessings received from above,*
*Most precious of all is the great gift of love.*

Iris Hesselden.

YOU'RE in a tight corner and you don't know which way to turn. The easiest course is to do nothing, wait and see what happens. There is another way, though.

It's called a try-angle. And you should make a straight line for it!

# THE FRIENDSHIP BOOK

WEDNESDAY—AUGUST 20.

OUR friend Mary enjoys a good cup of tea, and she was apologetic when the Lady of the House and I called to visit her.

"I'm afraid I'll have to make our refreshments with tea bags this afternoon," she explained. "I needed a new strainer and, perhaps unwisely, I was persuaded to buy one at the door, for the handle snapped off in no time at all. It's about as much use as a chocolate fireguard."

How we chuckled on the way home at what she had said. I have no doubt that from now on, "a chocolate fireguard" will be a very useful addition to the vocabulary in our household!

THURSDAY—AUGUST 21.

SITTING on the beach during our Summer holiday, I was fearful of the power shown by the huge waves crashing on the shore in such a fury. However, a week later, I sat at the same spot and what a difference there was!

The sea was calm and colourful and little waves broke entrancingly on the shore. What a change from a week before, and I couldn't help thinking how like life that picture was. Sometimes we are fearful of what is going to happen next, and think that things will never be right again.

However, one thing is certain — every storm eventually blows itself out, and if we are experiencing a miserable period we can be sure that, in time, our circumstances will improve.

PACK UP
YOUR TROUBLES

# THE FRIENDSHIP BOOK

FRIDAY—AUGUST 22.

TIME is one of those things that many of us complain we never have enough of!

I arrived for my weekly game of chess with my friend George just as his young visitor was leaving. Chris is a student, and always in a rush.

"Sorry I have to dash," he said, "but if I don't get back, I'll be up till midnight with this essay."

"That's all right, Chris," I said. "It's been nice to see you again."

However, as he saw his young grandson to the door, I heard George saying quietly, "Never say you don't have enough time. You have been given exactly the same number of hours each day as were given to Michelangelo, Leonardo da Vinci, Louis Pasteur, Charles Dickens and Mother Teresa."

I smiled to myself. It's all a matter of our priorities, isn't it?


SATURDAY—AUGUST 23.

ONE of my neighbours, Harry, was up a ladder taking in his plums. He had two buckets, one brimming with good plums and the other containing a few bad ones.

"You know, they're just like folks," he said. "Sometimes all the ones close to a bad 'un have turned bad as well. Other times the ones round about a rotten plum are completely unaffected. Now, if I was a philosopher, I would make something of that!"

Harry, you *are* a philosopher.

# THE FRIENDSHIP BOOK

<u>SUNDAY—AUGUST 24.</u>

O CLAP your hands, all ye people; shout unto God with the voice of triumph.

Psalms 47:1

<u>MONDAY—AUGUST 25.</u>

JUST the other day I heard myself saying to a friend, who had phoned to invite us to spend a day with her, "We would love to come, but not on a Monday, because on Mondays we always . . ."

Isn't it easy to get set in our habits of doing and thinking, in both the big and the little things in life? Another friend of ours says, "How I hate change! I like routine and things to stay the same."

That isn't the way of the world, though, is it?

Confucius, the great Chinese philosopher, teacher, and writer, who died in Shantung in 478 BC, had something to say on the matter all these years ago — "They must often change who would be constant in happiness and wisdom."

By the way, we spent a lovely Monday with our friend!

<u>TUESDAY—AUGUST 26.</u>

MAKE for a better tomorrow — by making the first effort today.

*Be cheery, not dreary.*
*Be happy, not sad.*
*Be carefree, despair free.*
*Begin now — be glad.*

# THE FRIENDSHIP BOOK

VISITING our friend Bill in an old people's home, I found the residents happily unpacking packets of sweets, chocolates and biscuits, from a box on the table. "Is this a special day?" I asked.

"Very special, at least to the givers," Bill replied.

Twice a year a box of goodies is brought to the home, all from one family. The people in question had decided on a different memorial to their parents, something they felt that their loved ones would have delighted in, and so on their parents' birthdays, the family clubs together, goes shopping, and these special boxes are the result.

What a lovely way to remember others, and to share an enduring love, too.

## TOO MUCH TO DO

*MY Dad had a saying I turn to,*
*When there is too much to be done,*
*For there are children to feed,*
*A garden to weed,*
*A kitchen to clean —*
*It's chaos indeed.*
*He said I should always remember,*
*To think when the going gets tough,*
*There is just one thing worse*
*Than too much to do,*
*And that is not having enough.*

Jean Harris.

# WHERE NEXT?

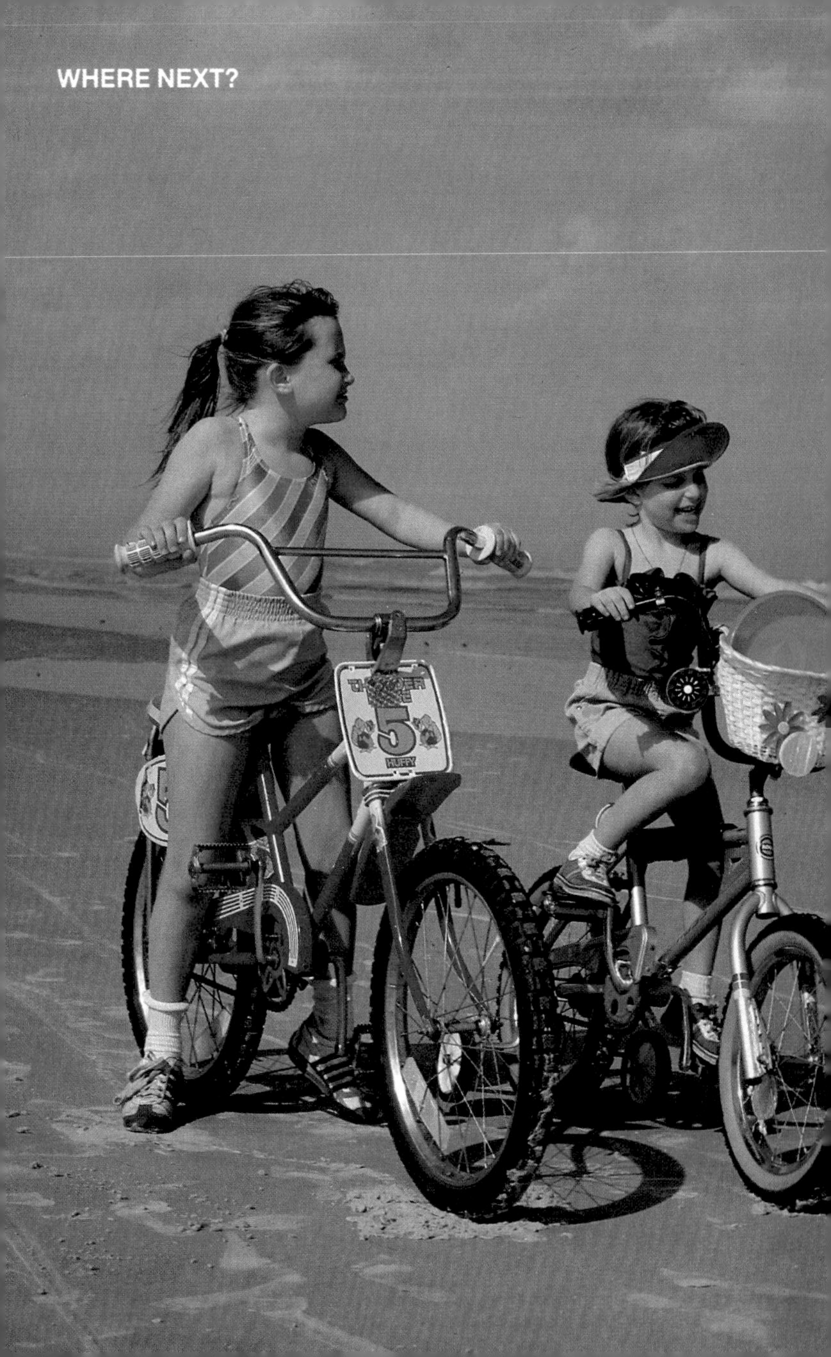

# THE FRIENDSHIP BOOK

THERE'S a lot of truth in the old sayings "Silence is golden" and "Least said, soonest mended", but have you heard the story about the young man who thought he would like to become a Trappist monk? It is a silent order, and so at the end of his first year he was called to the Abbot and allowed to say two words.

"I'm cold," said the young man.

"Go back and reflect again," said the Abbot.

At the end of another year the monk came before the Abbot again, for his two words.

"I'm hungry," he said.

Once again he was sent back for reflection.

At the end of the third year he was asked what he wished to say.

"I'm off," was the reply.

"Well, I'm not at all surprised," said the Abbot. "All the time you have been here you have done nothing but complain."

I LIKE the Greek Proverb, which says: — "Sorrow lasts longer than joy — if you let it."

BELOVED, follow not that which is evil, but that which is good. He that doeth good is of God: but he that doeth evil hath not seen God.

John III 1:11

# September

## MONDAY—SEPTEMBER 1.

ANN and George were telling us about their visit to a sheep fair in the North of England. Keen breeders were showing their best animals, and prizes were being awarded.

Ann was surprised that no one was acknowledging the prizewinners, so with a nudge to George, she began to clap. George followed suit, a polite ripple of applause followed, then everyone joined in.

It doesn't take much effort in everyday life to start the applause, does it? A word of appreciation for a little kindness done is applause indeed. The Book of Proverbs has a verse which sums it up perfectly:

"A word fitly spoken is like apples of gold in pictures of silver."

## TUESDAY—SEPTEMBER 2.

HERE are some wise words from my collection to think about today:

Life's like a clock —
No room for gloom on the face,
Much better to put a smile on the dial.

AUTUMN WONDER

# THE FRIENDSHIP BOOK

<u>WEDNESDAY—SEPTEMBER 3.</u>

A T the start of another school year I watched the children go down the road. Some were infants going on their very first day; some were juniors, confidently striding along; and some were older boys and girls, proudly setting off in their new secondary school uniforms.

I was reminded of a story about visitors to an ancient city who asked to be taken to meet the guardians there. First of all they were taken to the palace, but the visitors indicated that it was not what they intended. Then they headed for the military headquarters, but again the visitors said, "No, these are not the guardians of the city."

"Well, who *do* you want to see?" asked the people.

"Take us to the teachers," was the reply. "*They* are the guardians of the city."

Somebody once said that if you are a teacher you are eternal, for what you are and what you do lives on in the children that pass through your hands. So today, I salute teachers for all the valuable marks they make upon a child's mind, which time will never erase.

<u>THURSDAY—SEPTEMBER 4.</u>

I LIKE this thought very much, although I'm sorry that I don't know who wrote it:—

"The measure of what you can do for the world is the measure of what you let God do with you yourself."

# THE FRIENDSHIP BOOK

FRIDAY—SEPTEMBER 5.

HOW is your harvest this year? No, I am not talking about crops in the fields, but the flowers in your garden. You see, I have been reading the book "Perfume From Provence", Lady Fortescue's delightful account of her life in this French region before the Second World War.

At that time French scent factories looked to smallholders and farmers for their flower supplies, so she and her neighbours gathered in one crop after another — violets in February and March, then orange blossom and jessamine, followed by lavender, rosemary and others.

Somehow, just thinking of flowers as a crop has given them a new value in my eyes. They won't be used to make perfume, but they will spread it anyway and give pleasure with their beauty. So they certainly won't be wasted, will they?

SATURDAY—SEPTEMBER 6.

WRITER, broadcaster, and lecturer — Sir Compton Mackenzie was all those things, and one of his most popular novels "Whisky Galore" was made into the famous film of that name.

One of his most memorable remarks, though, is the simple statement: "If I were a godfather, wishing a gift on a child, it's that he should always be more interested in other people than in himself. That is a real gift."

A gift for life, I'd say.

# THE FRIENDSHIP BOOK

HE shall feed his flock like a shepherd: he shall gather the lambs with his arm and carry them in his bosom.

Isaiah 40:11

HERE is a quotation I jotted down in my little book. Actress Ingrid Bergman once said: "I stay so happy because I have a terrible memory."

Many things deserve to be remembered, and ought to be remembered. But life certainly is so much happier for us all, if we learn to forget the *unkind* things others have said or done to us.

I HEARD something said one day which I thought rather strange. A minister standing outside his church looked at a poster on the notice-board and said, "I must apologise for that!"

The poster carried the simple message: "Live each day as if it were your last."

Then he went on, "I must say 'Sorry' to the Lord for that one. It did not strike me at the time I put it up, but it is quite unnecessarily gloomy. I think we ought to start again and have another printed, saying, 'Live each day as if it were your first!' "

A more striking and also a much more positive way of thinking!

SEPTEMBER SPLENDOUR

# THE FRIENDSHIP BOOK

## WEDNESDAY—SEPTEMBER 10.

I ONCE attended a beautiful Harvest Festival weekend organised by our church, and I will always remember it.

At the Harvest Supper everyone was glowing with Christian friendship and companionship. The men had worked together to clear the machinery from a large barn, while the women had provided the delicious spread of buffet food. In spite of all this, however, something was missing.

An elderly member of our congregation realised what the problem was and we were all rather ashamed of ourselves — we had started eating without saying grace. Margaret, in spite of her frailness, tapped loudly on the table asking for silence so that grace might be said.

A lesson for us all that will never be forgotten.

## THURSDAY—SEPTEMBER 11.

IT always amazes me how much we can learn from a rainbow. I was reading the other day that when we move, the rainbow moves with us. We see a different reflection of the sun made by different raindrops as soon as we move. Someone standing next to us will see the colours differently, because they see a slightly different reflection.

So, if you ever see a certain situation differently from a friend, don't argue as to who is right — think of the rainbow instead and you may find that you are both right, but just seeing a slightly different reflection on the matter.

# THE FRIENDSHIP BOOK

FRIDAY—SEPTEMBER 12.

" I'M very fond of dandelions," my friend Peter remarked, as we gazed at his overgrown garden. "I don't understand why people hate them so much."

"Well, they are a weed, you know," I replied as tactfully as possible.

He pondered for a moment, looked thoughtful, and then addressed me again.

"Francis," he said, "who do you suppose originally decided which flowers were weeds and which were not?"

He continued: "Daisies are beautiful, but people get upset if they appear in the middle of their lawns. And what about buttercups? I love the bright yellow colour. Best of all, though, are dandelions."

On the way home later, I began to think about people, and how we have preconceived notions about who is good or who is not. I can't help feeling too many flowers have been cast as weeds!


SATURDAY—SEPTEMBER 13.

WHEN life is full of worries and money scarce, we sometimes find it very easy to make excuses and avoid doing things. Here are some wise words from the late Lord Stamp:

"It is easy to dodge our responsibilities but we cannot dodge the consequences of dodging our responsibilities."

Just think about it.

# THE FRIENDSHIP BOOK

## SUNDAY—SEPTEMBER 14.

**B**UT the path of the just is as the shining light, that shineth more and more unto the perfect day.

Proverbs 14:18

## MONDAY—SEPTEMBER 15.

### TRUE WEALTH

*W*HEN *you've counted all your money*
    *And stashed away each pound,*
*And told yourself there never is*
    *Enough to go around —*
*That's the time to tally up*
    *The things you get for free,*
*The sunlight and a baby's smile,*
    *The shade beneath a stately tree.*
*Unlike your wealth, they're always there*
    *For rich and poor alike to share.*

Kathleen M. Clark.

## TUESDAY—SEPTEMBER 16.

**A** TEACHER friend shared an amusing incident with me. One Autumn term he was asked, in an emergency, to teach a little history which was not his main subject. He thought he had better admit frankly to the boys at the outset that, in particular, he had never been very good at dates.

So, thoughtfully, when Christmas came round, the class bought him . . . a box of dates!

# THE FRIENDSHIP BOOK

<u>WEDNESDAY—SEPTEMBER 17.</u>

ALFRED WAINWRIGHT was a quiet, solitary man who never sought fame, but who found it through the exquisite publications he left as a legacy to other fell lovers, a series of seven guide books to the Lakeland Fells.

Born in Blackburn, Lancashire, he moved as soon as possible to work in the Borough Treasurer's office in Kendal, an ideal location for someone who had a lifelong love of the Lake District. It was there on the 9th November 1952 that he put pen to paper and began what was to take every minute of his spare time for the next 13 years.

He lived till he was 84, still overjoyed with the privilege of living amid such beauty.

"There is beauty everywhere: in the humble daisy, in the dappling of sunlight in woodland glades, in the clouds — everywhere. There are the miracles of renewal, sunset marking the end of a day and dawn heralding the start of another . . . We live in a magical fairyland and it is given to us to enjoy as an absolute gift. You do not need money in your pocket to walk through a field of wild flowers or on a heather moor . . . We have more blessings than we could ever count."

How true. What a wonderful world it is!

<u>THURSDAY—SEPTEMBER 18.</u>

I ONCE came across this Turkish proverb, and jotted it down. It says: "Who seeks a friend without a fault remains without one."

GOLDEN
MOMENTS

# THE FRIENDSHIP BOOK

## FRIDAY—SEPTEMBER 19.

"YOU should never ask an old person how they are," said an elderly acquaintance when I greeted her the other day. "They will always tell you!"

## SATURDAY—SEPTEMBER 20.

RECENTLY I was considering the old proverb: "Great oaks from little acorns grow."

It occurred to me that the art of printing owes its origin to impressions taken from letters carved on bark from a beech tree.

Gunpowder was discovered as the result of a spark falling on some materials mixed in a mortar.

The discovery of electricity stemmed from Michael Faraday observing that a piece of rubbed glass attracted small bits of paper.

Galileo noticed the lamp hanging in a church swinging to and fro — and this led to the invention of the pendulum clock.

The children of a maker of spectacles were playing with pieces of glass one day, and as they put one in front of another, they found that some far-away objects were beginning to appear quite close — and that led to the invention of the telescope.

Nearly all the big things in the world have grown from small beginnings. As a sentence underlined in an old biography dated 1862 says: "If we do every little thing that comes to us, God may out of our many littles make a great whole."

# THE FRIENDSHIP BOOK

## SUNDAY—SEPTEMBER 21.

GREAT is our Lord, and of great power: his understanding is infinite.

Psalms 147:5

## MONDAY—SEPTEMBER 22.

THE daily weather forecast is a must for one of our neighbours, and most of us know that the first thing she does each morning is to look out of the bedroom window, for what she sees determines what she will do with her day — washing, cleaning windows, gardening, or a day at the shops, perhaps.

However, she was a little taken aback when her husband presented her with a mysterious parcel containing a new tea-towel printed with these words:

*Hang outside the window and check each morning:*
*If it's wet, it's raining,*
*If it's stiff, it's freezing,*
*If it's white, it's snowing,*
*If it's moving, it's windy,*
*If it's faded, it's sunny,*
*If it's gone, it's been stolen!*

## TUESDAY—SEPTEMBER 23.

"CIVILITY costs nothing . . . except the effort." And how very much worthwhile it is to make that effort — it may have far-reaching effects on those with whom we come into contact.

# THE FRIENDSHIP BOOK

I WAS snipping off the dead blossoms from my rose bushes and thinking of a dear friend who died a couple of years ago. She loved roses.

One day, Janet and I had been discussing the bushes. "You know, those suckers are like us, always shooting off in every direction," she said, "and the twigs are the bitty bits of life that stop progress and slow us up."

"What about the thorns?" I asked.

"Handle them, like some awkward people, with kid gloves, and you'll be fine."

I recall her bending to smell a lovely blossom.

"Is that bloom the fulfilment of all our efforts and dreams?" I said.

"Oh, no," came back a firm and prompt reply, "it's our reward for all the care and attention we've given the plant."

"As you sow, so shall you reap," I quoted, and we both laughed.

Yes, it is sad when a close friend leaves us, but if you can recall the many happy and helpful things they said and did, and the good times shared, then they never really leave us, do they? We have them locked in our heart for ever.

I VERY much like the words written by D. W. Thompson: —

"I'd rather have an honest blockhead than a clever knave."

# THE FRIENDSHIP BOOK

ARE you daunted by a task which lies in front of you? Like the friend who said to us the other day: "I really don't know where to begin, but that's the only way to get finished."

He was surely remembering the Chinese proverb: "The man who removes a mountain begins by removing small stones."

## SHARING LOVE

*IF you have love to give and share,*
*Don't hide your love away,*
*But let it shine like morning sun*
*To cheer a cloudy day.*

*If you have love within your heart,*
*A bright, eternal flame,*
*You have a gift for all the world,*
*A message to proclaim.*

*If you can feel compassion now*
*Towards your fellow man,*
*Send out your caring, loving thoughts*
*As often as you can.*

*If you have God to walk with you*
*Just listen for His voice,*
*He gives His love for you to share,*
*Go forward and rejoice.*

Iris Hesselden.

# THE FRIENDSHIP BOOK

<u>SUNDAY—SEPTEMBER 28.</u>

FOR he that is mighty hath done to me great things; and holy is his name.

Luke 1:49

<u>MONDAY—SEPTEMBER 29.</u>

ARE you feeling put out because things aren't going your way? Well, perhaps these words will make you reflect:-

"Give and Take is the best double-act in life's show."

<u>TUESDAY—SEPTEMBER 30.</u>

OUR friend Mary was looking particularly happy when we visited her. The reason was that her young friend Helen had called in on her way from college.

"She wasn't able to stay long," said Mary, "but she is so enthusiastic and interested in everything that it is like a breath of fresh air blowing in and sweetening everything."

I knew exactly what Mary meant. There's always something new and interesting to see, even in the familiar and everyday, if we look hard enough.

It could be an unexpected visit, a rainbow after the rain, a bed of red roses in a neighbour's garden or a baby's first steps. Whatever it may be, let's take pleasure in all the good things around us and keep them safe in our storehouse of happy memories.

# October

WEDNESDAY—OCTOBER 1.

WHEN my small friend visited me recently, I remarked that I felt the cold very much these days.

"Oh, Mr Gay, will I knit you a cardigan?" Nicky asked.

As she's only five I thought this was a bit beyond her capabilities, but when I said, "I don't think you could manage to make a cardigan yet," she replied eagerly, "Oh, yes I could! I've already made Mummy an egg cosy!"

I couldn't help thinking what a pity more folk don't aspire to "making a cardigan" — even if to date they have only managed an "egg cosy".

THURSDAY—OCTOBER 2.

THE Golden Wedding celebrations of George and Isabel were a real success. When she was asked about her recipe for a happy marriage, Isabel smiled lovingly at her husband and said with a twinkle:

"I spend just a few minutes each week telling him how much I love him — and the rest of the time proving it."

# THE FRIENDSHIP BOOK

FRIDAY—OCTOBER 3.

WHEN Heather first retired it was "one long holiday," she told me gleefully. It was a different story, though, when I met her again six months later. "The holiday's over," she sighed. "I'll go crackers if I don't *do* something!"

So do something she did. She formed a club of over-sixties to meet in her home regularly for coffee and chat. They called themselves The Peppercorn Club.

Heather discovered that just a regular pleasant get-together wasn't enough — for herself, or the friends she'd gathered. They needed more aim, more purpose, so they turned themselves into a fund-raising group, deciding on the cause they should support for a year, and then going all out to raise as much money as they could.

They had such fun in their determined efforts, that quite soon a second club had to be formed . . . indeed, I've just heard a whisper that yet another club is on the way! I'm thinking they'll soon have to rename themselves — The Acorn Club — after the saying "Great oaks from little acorns grow".

Life *needs* some depth to it — just amusing and entertaining yourself is not enough.


SATURDAY—OCTOBER 4.

MY grandfather was not a man who ever wanted to get revenge for some real or imagined wrong done to him. As he used to say: "When you try to get even, it gets even worse."

# THE FRIENDSHIP BOOK

THE next day John seeth Jesus coming unto him, and saith, Behold the Lamb of God, which taketh away the sin of the world.

John 1:29

FEELING a bit down in the dumps today? Perhaps these words will raise your spirits:

"Life can be colourful — get rid of the blues, and you're in the pink."

WHENEVER the Lady of the House and I return home by train and see the shape of familiar hills in the distance, we know that the next station will be ours — and how welcome is the prospect of being safely home.

Those at sea must be continually thankful for the beams of lighthouses that keep them in safe waters, and how many travellers in the past, lost on lonely roads, have been guided to the shelter of a village by church towers and steeples?

All have been so important in guiding people along the way in a physical sense. When it comes to our emotional and spiritual journey, our friendly guides are to be found amongst our families and trusted friends, in our standards and beliefs, and within our faith or our church. Whatever would we do without them?

L

# THE FRIENDSHIP BOOK

THIS thought, written by Euripides so many years ago, is just as true today:

"It is a good thing to be rich, and a good thing to be strong, but it is a better thing to be beloved of many friends."

## SHIP-SHAPE

*THE sea of Life presents us*
*With some currents that confuse,*
*And many "ships" are needed*
*On this memorable cruise.*

*Apprentice-ship and Workman-ship*
*Can form a worthy crew,*
*Leader-ship and Statesman-ship*
*Can help steer us through.*

*Wor-ship is a Flag-ship*
*That is carefully designed,*
*And proper navigation*
*Can leave Hard-ship far behind.*

*Though the sea of Life's uncharted*
*At times, it must be said —*
*The finest craft is Friend-ship,*
*When it steams — Full Speed Ahead!*

John M. Robertson.

# THE FRIENDSHIP BOOK

FRIDAY—OCTOBER 10.

M Y friend Bertha gave up work to care for her elderly mother. When her mother died a few years later, she sold the house and went to live in a block of flats.

Everything seemed very strange in her new environment. Then something happened that filled her heart with hope and joy.

She had been shopping and had lost a five-pound note. Needing it badly, she told her neighbours in case they should find it. Well, that evening, several folk came to see her. Jack from next door, for instance, came to say he'd found the bank note — but Bertha refused it.

"Put it away, Jack. The young folk below brought me one they'd found, and then the widow on the ground floor found one, too; but do you know, *I* found the original money at the bottom of my carrier bag not long ago."

When Bertha thought that she had lost money, she was to discover that she had gained something far more precious — new, and caring, friends.


SATURDAY—OCTOBER 11.

T HESE two thoughts were sent to me by Elizabeth Gozney in Hertfordshire. Wise words, I think you'll agree:—

"If you speak your mind — mind what you speak!"

"Advice is like a repeat prescription — keep taking it daily!"

OCTOBER
LEAVES

# THE FRIENDSHIP BOOK

## SUNDAY—OCTOBER 12.

O GIVE thanks unto the Lord; for he is good; for his mercy endureth for ever.

Chronicles I 16:34

## MONDAY—OCTOBER 13.

A NNETTE was a little Jewish girl travelling with a group fleeing from Occupied France during the Second World War. They were on foot and she was exhausted when they reached the foothills of the Pyrenees. On the other side lay Spain and safety, but when she looked at the huge mountain in front of her, Annette despaired.

"I can never climb that!" she cried.

An older man spoke to her quietly. "You don't have to," he said. "All you have to do is take one step."

She took a step, then stood still.

"Now," he said, "take one more step."

So they went on. Taking it just one step at a time, Annette completed her arduous journey to freedom.

No matter how big a problem seems, or how huge an undertaking faces us, it becomes so much easier if we tackle it bit by bit, step by step, just like little Annette crossing the Pyrenees.

## TUESDAY—OCTOBER 14.

L IFE is like a game of cards . . . and stout hearts are always trumps.

# THE FRIENDSHIP BOOK

A FRIEND had once stayed for a weekend in the country.

"Did you enjoy the peace and quiet?" I asked on his return.

He chuckled for a moment and then remarked, "Francis, I had no idea the country could be so noisy!"

It seems that his room was close to a fast-flowing river and waterfall. Then rooks were nesting nearby, while the village clock chimed every hour. Church bells were rung early on Sunday morning.

A neighbouring farm had a number of "musical" cows that formed their own choir, accompanied by two young and enthusiastic dogs in the next garden. To add to this, my friend listened one night to a strange sound outside his bedroom door. It was only the following morning he realised that a Siamese cat lived in the house.

"So the noise of the traffic didn't bother you when you came home?" I asked, knowing that Jim lives near a busy main road.

"Not at all," he replied. "I slept like a baby."

Now, when I next read about a "dawn chorus", I'll think of my friend, and know that there is more to the countryside than meets the eye and the ear.

THERE'S a wise saying from the 18th-century writer Ben Johnson: "A man, Sir, should keep his friendship in constant repair."

# THE FRIENDSHIP BOOK

FRIDAY—OCTOBER 17.

HERE'S a quotation that gives food for thought: "An atheist is a man who has no visible means of support." — Lord Tweedsmuir.

SATURDAY—OCTOBER 18.

ONE of the doctors from our practice is a personal friend. She never discusses cases with me, of course, but one time I could see that something had amused her. It turned out that she had just paid a routine visit to an elderly gentleman and been shown a framed text above the mantelpiece.

"What do you think of that, Doctor?" she'd been asked. My friend, slightly taken aback, read the following words:

"The best doctors are Dr Diet, Dr Quiet and Dr Merryman."

She had laughed and replied that she had to agree.

As she drove away to continue her rounds, I considered what she had been saying. Though we do sometimes need medical attention, in a general sense these wise words still hold true. To eat sensibly and to sit quietly are good for both the body and the mind. We all know the value of laughter, which is a real tonic especially in times of stress.

I think I'd be pleased to have that text above my fireplace, too — a daily reminder of the best doctors available to each one of us!

# THE FRIENDSHIP BOOK

**SUNDAY—OCTOBER 19.**

THE Lord is my Shepherd; I shall not want.

Psalms 23:1

**MONDAY—OCTOBER 20.**

MANY people must remember the gale which swept across the south of England in 1987. Thousands of great trees were uprooted in one night and the whole countryside took on a new and devastated look.

The sight of those giant trees — some hundreds of years old — lying on the ground with their huge roots in the air is something southerners will never forget. It seemed at the time that it would take centuries to repair the damage — yet a few years later there was plentiful evidence of new growth.

The sunshine and air were able to penetrate the dense undergrowth for the first time in many decades, and this means that new plants are able to survive. New insects and many small animals have come to make their home here.

There is fresh life to be seen everywhere — a real triumph after disaster!

**TUESDAY—OCTOBER 21.**

I HAVE heard many descriptions of the difference between optimism and pessimism, but the one I like best is that the pessimist says, "Isn't it a pity that roses have thorns?", while the optimist says, "Isn't it wonderful that thorns have roses?"

# THE FRIENDSHIP BOOK

**WEDNESDAY—OCTOBER 22.**

OVER the fireplace at Arley Hall in Cheshire can be seen these words: "Hope Confidently; Do Valiantly; Wait Patiently".

I think they make quite an encouraging sermon in a nutshell — don't you?

**THURSDAY—OCTOBER 23.**

JOHN GREENLEAF WHITTIER was an American Quaker, humanitarian, champion of the anti-slavery cause and author of one of our best-loved hymns, "Dear Lord and Father of mankind, forgive our foolish ways."

Although Whittier's poem "Kind Words" was written more than 100 years ago, its message is just as relevant today:—

*A little word in kindness spoken,*
*    A motion or a tear,*
*May heal a spirit broken,*
*    And make a friend sincere.*

*A word, or look, has crushed to earth*
*    Oft many a budding flower,*
*Which, had a smile but owned its birth,*
*    Would have blest life's latest hour.*

*Then deem it not an idle thing*
*    A kindly word to speak;*
*The face you wear, the smile you bring,*
*    May soothe a heart or break.*

# THE FRIENDSHIP BOOK

PAT HARRIS, when president of that world-wide organisation, Mothers' Union, proved to be a lady of vision and practicality.

When the London headquarters of the M.U., named Mary Sumner House after its founder, was built more than 70 years ago, it was adequate for the times. Then urgent work became necessary to improve it.

As her contribution, Pat Harris undertook to create, in cross stitch, a map of the world showing where all the 16,500 branches of the Mothers' Union are located. In the piece of needlework measuring 36″ by 24″ and comprising 169,000 stitches, it was a task to keep her busy for months as she travelled by rail and air to visit the different branches. She hoped that members would help, too, for she said, "If each member would sponsor at least one stitch, Mary Sumner House could be transformed into the modern headquarters Mothers' Union deserves."

Now the finished tapestry can be seen at Mary Sumner House, Tufton Street, London. Each of us has a part to play in life — whether it be great or small — and the only thing that matters is how well we carry out our own part.

LOOKING through my mother's old autograph book I found a rather lovely verse. It said: "Life without laughter is like bread without yeast."

# THE FRIENDSHIP BOOK

SUNDAY—OCTOBER 26.

JESUS CHRIST the same yesterday, and today and forever.

Hebrews 13:8

MONDAY—OCTOBER 27.

TODAY I want to tell you what Michael Quoist once said:

"When you don't have enough time to get everything done, stop for a moment and pray."

Can you think of any better advice?

TUESDAY—OCTOBER 28.

THE Wilson family were all in different parts of the house when the lights went out. Teenage Tracy was up in her room listening to her kind of music. Her younger brother, Mark, was playing a video game in his den. Their father was watching television, while Mum was writing a letter.

When everything suddenly went black — a power failure caused by a storm — the family all gathered in the sitting-room.

"It was great," said Mrs Wilson to me afterwards. "I lit some candles and we just sat and chatted. We had a really good laugh. In fact, we were enjoying ourselves so much that we were quite sorry when the lights went on again!"

She told me they have decided to get together more often in the evenings. They have been looking out some old family games they used to play, and are looking forward to the long Winter nights.

# THE FRIENDSHIP BOOK

## WEDNESDAY—OCTOBER 29.

I FOUND this little item in a church magazine. I do not know who wrote it — just sit down quietly and think about it.

"A ready accuser is usually a self-excuser."

## THURSDAY—OCTOBER 30.

AS we were returning home from our walk, we met Doris at her gate a few doors along. She was waving goodbye to her daughter and three-year-old grandson.

Proudly, she told us how little Adam had suddenly put his arms around her neck that afternoon and said, "I love you, Grandma."

We knew that the memory would stay with her for many years. As we went indoors, I thought how rarely grown-ups say those words to each other.

How long is it since you told someone dear to you how much you cared for them? It takes only a moment, uses a few words, but what happiness is given!

Perhaps we can learn a lesson from that little boy and not be afraid to show our feelings. After all, isn't it love that makes the world go round?

## FRIDAY—OCTOBER 31.

IF you're feeling discouraged or just needing a positive thought for today, think about this saying:—

The best speed on the road of life is sixty smiles-per-hour.

# November

ANDY works in a large city office. He wears smart business clothes, but at lunchtime he changes into an old tracksuit and goes out for a run. One day, as he hurried through reception on his way out, he overheard a clerkess say, "No one should go out dressed like *that!*" Andy just smiled.

What the girl didn't realise is that Andy's mother is house-bound. She lives two miles from the office and every day Andy runs there just to check that she is well, then runs back to work.

He finds that the midday run helps ease the stress that can build up in his job, and his daily visit, though short, brightens up his mother's day much more than a phone call would do.

This story reminds us that we should never judge anyone by their outward appearance. It's only when we really get to know someone that we can find the goodness that is in so many people.

APPLY thine heart unto instruction, and thine ears to the words of knowledge.

Proverbs 23:12

# THE FRIENDSHIP BOOK

## START NOW

*I*F you want to be happy, then start right away,
*Doing a kindness for someone each day;*
*Scatter some sunshine, forget about self,*
*And put all your worries away on the shelf.*

THESE days much is said and written about the environment, and many of us try in our own way to make it cleaner and to preserve this world for coming generations.

There is a story told by Millais, the famous artist, of how he first saw the beauty of nature. His father was a countryman, and sometimes he would take him in the evening to sit near a cornfield to watch the rabbits scuttling hither and thither, and see the corn swaying in the breeze.

One evening there was a most beautiful sunset and he tells us that his elderly father stood up facing its splendour, took off his cap and said, "My son, it is God."

There would be no more desecration, destruction or pollution, if we would revere not only God — but his handiwork.

THE world's best medicine is laughter, to be taken in large doses.

# THE FRIENDSHIP BOOK

## SATURDAY—NOVEMBER 8.

GIVE and Take shared a house together. One day they set out on a long journey. Give strolled along, enjoying the walk, but Take was pushing a barrow laden with so many of his possessions that he could not keep up. His clothes, too, were weighed down by all the things in his pockets.

Give reached their destination, still as fresh as when they started. Take was so busy going back to pick up items he had dropped that he never got there. They say he is struggling along still, racked with worries and terrified of losing all his precious belongings.

## SUNDAY—NOVEMBER 9.

FOR the Lord God is a sun and shield: the Lord will give grace and glory; no good thing will he withhold from them that walk uprightly.

Psalms 84:11

## MONDAY—NOVEMBER 10.

OUR friend Ann called one day, and told us of a happy experience. She had taken a few flowers to an acquaintance to brighten up a dull Winter's day.

The next time they met, the lady who had received them said that she had appreciated the flowers so much it had inspired her to make the effort to take a bunch to one of *her* friends.

Truly a case of good spreading good.

M

# THE FRIENDSHIP BOOK

<u>TUESDAY—NOVEMBER 11.</u>

**H**AVEN'T we all met someone, who says of a personal ambition, "It's just a dream, there are too many difficulties to make it come true."

One person who did not say that of his cherished ambition was William Ross, a young Scottish farmworker, who wanted to be a minister. William was born in Errol last century, and grew up in beautiful Perthshire at Abernyte.

However, to be a minister William had to go to university, which meant money was needed to keep him there and pay his fees. To earn more money than he could on the farm, William became a joiner in Perth, and discovered he had a talent for woodwork.

Eventually, aged 30, William Ross became a student at St Andrews University. Eight years later he was ordained as a minister, and sailed for Africa to become a missionary. William had at last fulfilled his cherished ambition, having overcome many difficulties along the way.

It is surprising just how many apparently firmly closed doors in life open, if you just walk up to them and push hard.

<u>WEDNESDAY—NOVEMBER 12.</u>

**I** VERY much like the quotation which says: "God guard my memories for I know that the days will not always be as fair as these."

Memories are precious, more so the older one gets.

# THE FRIENDSHIP BOOK

## THURSDAY—NOVEMBER 13.

A FRIEND said to me, "Sometimes I feel like asking God why he allows so many evils in the world."

"Why don't you?" I asked.

"Because," said the man, "I'm afraid He will ask me the same question!"

## FRIDAY—NOVEMBER 14.

I ONCE came across a Teacher's Creed written in the autograph book of a young teacher in the 1920s. It went as follows:

*I believe in boys and girls, the men and women of a great tomorrow.*

*I believe in the curse of ignorance, in the dignity of teaching, in the joy of serving others.*

*I believe in wisdom, as revealed in human lives as well as in the pages of a printed book, in lessons taught not so much by precept as by example, in ability to work with the hands as well as think with the head.*

*I believe in beauty in the school room, the home and the great outdoors.*

*I believe in laughter, in love, in faith.*

*I believe we receive a just reward for all we are and all we do.*

*I believe in the present and its opportunities, in the future and its promises, in the divine joy of living.*

I reckon a teacher who can put all those precepts into practice must be a great teacher!

# THE FRIENDSHIP BOOK

## SATURDAY—NOVEMBER 15.

IN Thackeray's great novel "Vanity Fair" I came on this thought:—

"The world is a looking-glass, and gives back to every man the reflection of his own face. Frown at it, and it in turn will look sourly upon you; laugh at it and with it, and it is a jolly kind companion."

## SUNDAY—NOVEMBER 16.

HE revealeth the deep and secret things: he knoweth what is in the darkness, and the light dwelleth with him.

Daniel 2:22

## MONDAY—NOVEMBER 17.

ONE Winter I visited an old friend. "It's a pity you had to come at this time of year," she said, "when my garden is so bare."

A pity in one sense, yes, but her next words instantly stirred my imagination. "Oh, if only I could show you the daffodils and tulips, and the dainty little violets under the soil."

Suddenly, in that wonderful gift — the mind's eye — I saw, not wet brown earth, but bright golden daffodils waving in the breeze, and noble tulips standing sentinel over the tiny violets.

What a wonderful message of hope! Next time you look out of your window at the bare trees, empty flower tubs and borders, remember these words and let your imagination take root.

# THE FRIENDSHIP BOOK

SOMETIMES, when I sit reading, I think of some of the sayings and expressions connected with books. We speak about the end of a chapter, and of somebody's life being a closed book or, much better, an open one.

Best of all I like the phrase to turn over a new leaf, meaning a new page. It's good to know, when a story gets boring, that you can simply turn to the next page. Similarly, in life, we can at any time put the past behind us and start again with a clean sheet.

ONE morning Lady Elgar, wife of the famous composer, came downstairs to breakfast and heard the most beautiful sounds coming from the music room. She stopped and listened entranced as her husband played a melody she had never heard before. As soon as he had finished, she burst in and said, "What was that? It's wonderful!"

"Oh, it's only nonsense," he said. "I was merely passing the time until you came down to breakfast."

"You must publish it," she told him. "The public will love it."

They did. The "nonsense" Edward Elgar had composed that morning was "Land Of Hope And Glory".

To think that if his wife had not urged him to publish it, that great and inspiring melody might never have been heard again!

# THE FRIENDSHIP BOOK

A NEIGHBOUR of mine recently celebrated her eighty-fifth birthday, and Janet's family and friends gave her a splendid party. Somebody asked her what things she would have changed in her life if she could live it over again.

"If I could live these years over again," she said, "I'd make more mistakes, I would be sillier because I know very few things which should be taken seriously. I would have a few real problems, instead of lots of imaginary ones. I'd ride on more merry-go-rounds, and eat more ice-cream! Most of all I'd have lots of moments, one after another, instead of living my years ahead of each other and worrying about things which I couldn't change and which mostly didn't happen anyway."

Wouldn't it be nice to be as wise as that *before* we get to a ripe old age!

C OMPTON MACKENZIE'S first book was a failure. It was a collection of poems and nobody wanted to read them. He was living in Cornwall at the time and, deeply disappointed, wandered one dark night down to the seashore.

There a tiny light caught his eye. It was a glow-worm in the grass and to the young writer it seemed like a sign, urging him to try again. He did, and his next book, "The Passionate Elopement", made his name as a novelist. He never looked back — and all thanks to that little glow-worm!

# THE FRIENDSHIP BOOK

YOU may, or may not, agree with the methods used by Billy Graham for preaching his religion, but you must admit that he has influenced many thousands of people and done an enormous amount of good.

Yet Graham was once a non-believer. That was before he went to hear the preaching of Mordecai Ham, a non-conformist minister.

We are told that during the singing of the hymn "Just As I Am", Graham found new thoughts coming into his mind — thoughts that were eventually to change not only his whole life, but the lives of thousands of others worldwide.

Perhaps this story serves to remind us that we never know at what moment we may be called upon to change our way of life for a better one. So surely, we should all be ready to take up the challenge.

AND that from a child thou hast known the holy scriptures, which are able to make thee wise unto salvation through faith which is in Christ.

Timothy II 3:15

PATIENCE is an excellent virtue, but don't carry it too far or you will become one of those people who are like wheelbarrows — they stand still until they are pushed!

# THE FRIENDSHIP BOOK

## CHANCE MEETING

*C*OME, *hold me by the hand, dear friends,*
*Too long since our last meeting,*
*So many years to make amends,*
*So clasp my hands in greeting.*

*Why did we never keep in touch,*
*Why leave it much too late?*
*Such friends we were, and cared so much —*
*This meeting now is Fate.*

*We'll bridge the gap, the years between*
*And make a solemn vow,*
*That Time no more will intervene*
*To spoil our friendship now.*

Dorothy M. Loughran.

IT had been one of those weeks, when anything that could go wrong *went* wrong. Nothing really serious, however, thank goodness! But as the Lady of the House said, we enjoyed — if that is the right word — "a heap of irritation".

Certainly that week we temporarily mislaid our sense of humour, and forgot the wise words of that writer of good stories, William Makepeace Thackeray, the author of "Vanity Fair":

"A good laugh is sunshine in a house."

**AT THE END
OF THE DAY**

# THE FRIENDSHIP BOOK

A GREAT preacher and a great sermon need only one thing more: great listeners.

B ROTHER LAWRENCE was born in France in the 17th century, and when he was 18 had a dramatic conversion experience.

He served as a young soldier in the Thirty Years War, and received an injury to his leg which left him with a permanent limp. However, it gave him the opportunity of following his calling to enter the Carmelite monastery in Paris.

He was put to work in the kitchen where he described himself as "a great awkward fellow who broke everything." With his dislike of cooking, his lameness and the pressure of working to prepare food for such a large community, he could have found the life irksome, yet he was blissfully happy.

People flocked to learn the secret of his serenity and peace, and Lawrence told them, "The time of business does not differ with me from the time of prayer; and in the noise and clatter of my kitchen, while several persons are at the same time calling for different things, I possess God in as great tranquillity as if I were on my knees."

The story of Brother Lawrence reminds me of another busy person — the housewife who put a card on the wall above her kitchen sink:

*DIVINE SERVICE HELD HERE*
*THREE TIMES DAILY*

# THE FRIENDSHIP BOOK

IS there anything more precious in this world than a close family bond? However, there are so many children nowadays who have no *full* experience of it, such as Mickey and his little sister, Eileen. Their father works on an oil rig in the North Sea, and he is often away from home for weeks on end.

Now, you might think that these lengthy periods of separation would loosen family ties — but not a bit of it, because on the mantelshelf in the living-room stands a huge smiling photo of their father. Every night at bed-time — without fail — the children look up at him and say goodnight, and sometimes they even relate something special that has happened during the day. Around the time he knows his children will be going to bed, their father pauses to look at the photo he has of them all in his wallet, and whispers a goodnight.

He, strangely enough, seems to know all about the happenings they tell his photo, and he even mentions them when he writes and when he gets home. Of course, their mother is a good letter-writer, so maybe she has something to do with it!

Happy are the children who know the love and care of their parents — a bond which is a prize beyond all riches.

HE maketh my feet like hinds' feet, and setteth me upon my high places.

Psalms 18:33

# December

## MONDAY—DECEMBER 1.

THE Lady of the House and I were enjoying our morning cup of coffee, when she said to me, "Do you know what Margaret told me yesterday? 'You hold most fast to loved ones by gently letting them go.' "

I thought I would share Margaret's wise words with you. They make a good thought for today, and all our tomorrows.

## TUESDAY—DECEMBER 2.

A WRITER, asked to speak to a hall full of school children, gave these three pieces of advice:

Set out to be tough *and* tender. If you're just tender, a mouse can walk all over you. But if you're just tough, you will become a brute.

Always honour your friendships.

Show courtesy because your words may be the only kind thing a person hears all day.

Wise advice . . . but for young children only? It struck me that it was excellent advice for grown-up children also! Don't you agree?

# THE FRIENDSHIP BOOK

AT the beginning of December, we are usually invited to stay with farmer friends who live in the Cotswolds.

It is delightful to see them, and we have long chats in the evening by their large log fire, exchanging all the news of the past year.

We have long early morning walks, too, breathing in the fresh air, seeing the ploughed fields so brown and straight — like corduroy. What we enjoy most, though, is our visit to the village church on our way back to the farm.

It is always so quiet at that time of day, as we walk on tip-toe down the aisle to peep at the crib by the altar. Nobody whispering, no nativity play, no carol singing — just peace. A special peace that we can always carry with us into another year.

DAPHNE DU MAURIER was one of the most successful novelists of her time. Her private life, however, was scarred by spells of deep unhappiness and anxiety. Tragedy touched her more than once. She survived it all with humility and a deep inner strength, and nothing demonstrates her courage more than these words written in a letter to an old friend:—

"I think the thing is always to look ahead in life, and never look back, except in gratitude for happy times past."

Sound advice we could all take.

# THE FRIENDSHIP BOOK

## FRIDAY—DECEMBER 5.

ONE very wet December morning the Lady of the House looked through our window and remarked how long it seemed before the roses would bloom again.

When I got home that evening after visiting a friend who had flu, I found the Lady of the House smiling. Fresh flowers had been arranged in the hall. She told me that during the morning she decided that she must be bright and optimistic, in spite of the weather, and had gone to the florist's to bring sunnier days a little nearer.

Whatever the season, the marvels of nature are all around us — if only we choose to find them.

## SATURDAY—DECEMBER 6.

I REMEMBER once quoting the enigmatic words of Ralph Waldo Emerson, the American lecturer, essayist and poet:—

"Though we travel the world over to find the beautiful, we must carry it with us or we find it not."

"What do you mean?" I was asked. "What must we carry with us to find the beautiful?"

Surely the eyes and the desire to see, as demonstrated by the overheard conversation below.

"It is so badly drawn, and the perspective is all wrong," said a visitor to an art exhibition speaking of a painting.

"Yes, I agree," said his companion, "but aren't the colours wonderfully bright and beautiful?"

# THE FRIENDSHIP BOOK

## SUNDAY—DECEMBER 7.

A ND she shall bring forth a son, and thou shalt call his name Jesus: for he shall save his people from their sins.

Matthew 1:21

## MONDAY—DECEMBER 8.

E LEANOR ROOSEVELT was a great support to her American President husband. I have found a thought of hers that can help us all. She said: "No one can diminish you without your consent."

## TUESDAY—DECEMBER 9.

S OME time during the Twelve Days of Christmas the Lady of the House and I always have a little supper party for one or two old friends. Nothing elaborate, you know, just a simple help-yourself buffet, with coffee and mince pies to follow for everyone to enjoy round the fire.

We pull crackers, wear paper hats and inevitably we take a trip down memory lane, which is much enjoyed by our guests for we all went to school together. Of course we could meet and have a meal in a hotel; it would be less trouble, but somehow it would not be the same as being at home with your friends.

As Cicero, the great Roman statesman, philosopher, and orator said: "No place is more delightful than one's own fireside."

A HINT
OF WINTER

M

# THE FRIENDSHIP BOOK

"SILENCE is golden," says the proverb. At times, true — but speech is of greater value even than gold. It is the great communicator — it shares ideas, imparts wisdom, corrects ignorance and prejudices, and above all it lessens the loneliness of the lonely.

Go and speak to someone — NOW if possible. If they're lonely, it will lighten their burden and uplift their spirit, and if *you* are lonely, then "just speaking" will do the same for you.

AT Christmas the junior section of our local drama group stages a children's play. We never miss it because it is always such good fun.

One year they attempted "The Wizard Of Oz". The costumes were very effective — the Tin Man's suit glistened in the footlights as he reminded us of our need for big, kind, loving hearts, while the wicked witch cackled under her tall black hat as she produced her spells from a shopping trolley!

These young people are not in the running for Olivier Awards, but there is an honesty about their acting plus a pleasure in what they are communicating. This is something that cannot be taught.

As you go around each day, have you noticed the people who are honest and conscientious in their daily work? I have, they are usually the ones with the big, kind, loving hearts.

# THE FRIENDSHIP BOOK

*GOODBYE to the days of rushing,*
*A slave to the dictates of time*
*And the constant demands of the phone's ring,*
*Retirement is quite sublime.*

*So you think, as you laze in an armchair*
*And dream of the things you might do —*
*The books you might read, the friends you might meet,*
*The hobbies you might pursue.*

*You promise yourself that some day*
*You will try to tackle them all.*
*Some day when you feel in the mood — but then*
*You glance at the clock on the wall,*

*And suddenly time still matters.*
*You realise this IS "some day"*
*And you'd better get moving, for that old clock*
*Is ticking your life away!*

Elspeth P. Vincent.

"CLEANLINESS", so the old saying goes, "is next to godliness." However, I prefer to think that friendship is next to godliness.

I don't think God minds very much if we are not scrupulously clean every moment of the day, but he does mind if we are not scrupulously kind.

So let us forget the smudge on our faces and put a smile there instead.

# THE FRIENDSHIP BOOK

I AM come a light into the world, that whosoever believeth on me should not abide in darkness.

John 12:46

GENERAL EVA BURROWS, one-time leader of the Salvation Army, recalled a nativity play in Zimbabwe when she was a mission teacher there.

There were eight angels. Six of the eight were black, the exceptions being the blonde daughters of a Norwegian couple who also worked at the mission station.

During a pause in dress rehearsal, Eva Burrows overheard one of the blonde Norwegians ask her sister: "Do you think there will be black angels in Heaven?"

"Of course there will!" replied her sister, adding with lovely insight, "And anyhow, Jesus would not know the difference."

HERE is a Christmastide wish for us all from the pen of Charles Dickens, the author of that well-loved tale "A Christmas Carol". He wrote to John Forster, his long-time friend and biographer, "Many merry Christmases, friendships, great accumulation of cheerful recollections, affection on earth, and Heaven at last for all of us."

Have a festive season both happy and merry!

# THE FRIENDSHIP BOOK

## WEDNESDAY—DECEMBER 17.

I CAME across the silk-tasselled book mark tucked carefully inside the family Bible, passed down to me for safe-keeping. On it are hand sewn, in painstaking cross-stitch, the words: "Every cloud has a silver lining".

I wondered who in the family had stitched this prescription for a cheerful outlook on life, in neat crosses in red, black, and yellow wools.

Today, both family history societies and genealogical research flourish. There is something comforting about the past and the present going hand in hand; it gives a continuity and pattern to life, don't you think?

## THURSDAY—DECEMBER 18.

CANDLES are fashionable and attractive Yuletide decorations.

Our ancestors sometimes used the candle as an alternative to the Yule Log. Lighting it at dawn on Christmas Day, it would burn till midnight, ensuring prosperity and luck. In Ireland the Christmas Candle is usually a large red one, decorated with holly. Standing in a scooped-out turnip, it is placed in the main window on Christmas Eve to guide the Holy Family to shelter.

Our churches are often decked with greenery and lit with candles on Christmas Eve. The Christian Church uses candles to represent Christ, the light of the world. Can there be any more welcoming sight at this time of year?

A CRISP TROT

# THE FRIENDSHIP BOOK

## FRIDAY—DECEMBER 19.

I'VE seen Christmas trees with a fairy at the top and also with a Santa Claus, but the most curious custom of all must be in Labrador where they use a dried cod's head. Apparently, that is regarded as a very special luxury there.

However, I always feel that the best thing of all at the top of the tree is a star; the authentic Christmas symbol, the centre of the story of the visit of the Wise Men from the East to the Christ Child.

The important thing is not just to get the right thing at the top of the Christmas tree, but, so to speak, to get the right thing at the top of Christmas itself. It is so easy to concentrate on parties, presents and all the other trimmings and to forget that at the top of the list should be the spiritual message of Christmas — the difference that the coming of Jesus made to our world.

## SATURDAY—DECEMBER 20.

HE'S a cheerful soul, the man I often greet with a few friendly words when we meet buying our morning papers. Rain or shine you can almost hear a smile in his voice. It seems to make the day a little brighter.

In this I am reminded of the words that Joseph Addison, the famous essayist, wrote in "The Spectator" on 17th May 1712: "Cheerfulness keeps up a kind of daylight in the mind and fills it with a steady and perpetual serenity."

# THE FRIENDSHIP BOOK

GLORY to God in the highest, and on earth peace, good will toward men.

Luke 2:14

A YOUNG man once set out determined to be a hero and fight great battles. He rode a long way but encountered no enemy. His sword grew rusty. Then one day he found a helpless leper, alone and friendless.

In an instant the young man knew that the enemy he had to conquer was the fear of the afflicted such as this, the victory he had to win was over disease and poverty. He leaped from his horse and embraced the leper.

This was the first noble deed of St Francis of Assisi, the friend of the poor and outcast.

IT was the school Nativity play.

One of the lads had fallen for the little girl who had been cast in the part of Mary, and he desperately wanted to play the part of Joseph. He was most put out, therefore, when he was given the comparatively minor role of the innkeeper.

However, all was not lost.

When Joseph and Mary knocked on his door to enquire whether he had any room, he replied cheerfully, "You can come in, Mary — but you can buzz off, Joe!"

# THE FRIENDSHIP BOOK

WEDNESDAY—DECEMBER 24.

IT was the afternoon of a bustling Christmas Eve. All that morning the Lady of the House had been busy with last-minute preparations. Feeling rather relieved that everything was ready for the 25th, we carried our tea cups to the window-seat to enjoy a well-earned rest.

The day was still, not too cold and with no sign of a white Christmas. The clouds were already tinted pale pink and dusk was not too far away. As we sat gazing out, at peace with the world, we saw a butterfly! It flew straight to the glass, fluttered a moment almost as if it wanted us to admire its beautiful markings, then promptly disappeared.

"Well," said the Lady of the House, "what a delightful and unexpected Christmas gift!"

I agreed. Emerging from the chrysalis, the butterfly begins a reborn existence.

Perhaps that is what Christmas really is. Not just a time for celebrations and gifts, but a time of renewal, too. A new start and a new life.

THURSDAY—DECEMBER 25.

HAPPY Christmas!
We all chuckled last Christmas morning when our minister asked the children, "I wonder if anyone call tell me whose birthday it is today?"

A little hand shot up in the front row, and a young voice piped up, "I don't know whose birthday it is today, but it's *mine* tomorrow."

SWANSONG

# THE FRIENDSHIP BOOK

FRIDAY—DECEMBER 26.

THE finest ship to sail the sea of life is Friendship.

J. M. Robertson.

SATURDAY—DECEMBER 27.

JUST after Christmas one year, the Lady of the House and I were invited for coffee by an elderly couple who are good neighbours. They wanted us to see their Christmas present to each other.

We were ushered into their cosy sitting-room and there, in a corner, stood a magnificent CD player. As we drank coffee, they told us how much they enjoyed listening to music and now they could play it as often as they wished.

Ted and Jane had been married for 56 years. Quite an achievement in itself, but even more remarkable is their approach to life and their modern outlook. I thought of all the people who have no interest in music. So much is missing from their lives, for music can be either a tonic, a healing balm, or a source of happy memories.

As we made our farewells, I couldn't help thinking of that famous quotation: "If music be the food of love, play on."

SUNDAY—DECEMBER 28.

FOR God sent not his Son into the world to condemn the world; but that the world through him might be saved.

John 3:17

# THE FRIENDSHIP BOOK

<u>MONDAY—DECEMBER 29.</u>

S OME years ago there used to be a popular song of which I was very fond. I can't remember all the verses but I know the chorus went something like this:—

"I want to be happy but I can't be happy till I make you happy, too."

What a fine sentiment for this time of year. And if we can make somebody else happy, some of that happiness will surely rub off on ourselves.

<u>TUESDAY—DECEMBER 30.</u>

I HAVE just found this anonymous quotation. Think about it deeply because it means such a lot in this world of today:

"The day we stop burning with love people will die of the cold."

<u>WEDNESDAY—DECEMBER 31.</u>

A NOTHER year is drawing to a close. A time to forgive and forget, to put aside hurt and disappointment. A time to remember happy days and unexpected kindnesses. Perhaps, also, a time to make new resolutions, though most of us can find them difficult to keep. In the words of Tennyson:

*Ring out the old, ring in the new,*
*Ring, happy bells, across the snow:*
*The year is going, let him go;*
*Ring out the false, ring in the true.*

Don't be afraid to let the old year go, for a fresh New Year is waiting. May it hold health, happiness, love and friendship for each one of us.

# The Photographs

THE GOOD COMPANIONS — *Llyn Gwynant, North Wales.*
GLORY IN THE HIGHEST — *Down Ampney, near Cirencester.*
HIGH WATER — *Corpach, near Fort William.*
SAFE GRAZING — *Naunton Village, Cotswolds.*
TOWERS OF STRENGTH — *Tower Bridge, London.*
SPRING CRUISE — *Lake Windermere, near Ambleside.*
SAYING IT WITH FLOWERS — *Lotherton Hall, near Leeds.*
PEAK POWER — *Glen Coe.*
NATURE'S PAINTBRUSH — *The Langdales, from Elter Water.*
BLUE HAVEN — *Plockton, West Highlands.*
EVENING SHADES — *River Tay, at Perth.*
PEACEFUL PASTURES — *River Derwent, Derbyshire.*
TIME FOR REFLECTION — *Leeds And Liverpool Canal, Shipley.*
DEEP IN THOUGHT — *Tintagel coastline, Cornwall.*
JUST A BACK GARDEN — *Dunrobin Castle, near Dornoch.*
SOFT AND GLOW — *Bude, Cornwall.*
A PATH TO FOLLOW — *The Cotswold Way and St Eadburgh's Church, Broadway.*
SWANS — STONES — SERENITY — *Llyn Padarn, Gwynedd.*
NO WORRIES — *Lower Slaughter, Gloucestershire.*
PACK UP YOUR TROUBLES — *At Brimham Rocks, Yorkshire.*
WHERE NEXT? — *On the beach.*
AUTUMN WONDER — *A woodland walk.*
SEPTEMBER SPLENDOUR — *Stoford Village, Somerset.*
GOLDEN MOMENTS — *The Hermitage, Dunkeld.*
OCTOBER LEAVES — *Belfast Castle grounds.*
I'M ALL EARS — *Pembroke Welsh Corgi.*
AT THE END OF THE DAY — *Near Snowshill Village, Cotswolds.*
A HINT OF WINTER — *Snowdon and Capel Curig, Gwynedd.*
A CRISP TROT — *Ardington, Oxfordshire.*
SWANSONG — *River Windrush at Burford, Oxfordshire.*

ACKNOWLEDGEMENTS: **Andy Williams;** The Good Companions, Peak Power, Nature's Paintbrush, Swans — Stones — Serenity, Golden Moments. **Paul Felix;** Glory In The Highest, A Path To Follow, No Worries, At The End Of The Day, Swansong. **V. K. Guy;** High Water, Spring Cruise, Blue Haven, Evening Shades, Just a Back Garden, A Hint Of Winter. **Ivan J. Belcher;** Safe Grazing, Towers Of Strength, Peaceful Pastures, Deep In Thought, I'm All Ears, A Crisp Trot. **Clifford Robinson;** Saying It With Flowers, Soft and Glow, Pack Up Your Troubles. **J. Winkley;** Time For Reflection. **Picturepoint;** Where Next? **Kenneth Scowen;** Autumn Wonder, September Splendour. **Jim McCabe;** October Leaves.

Printed and Published by D. C. Thomson & Co., Ltd.,
185 Fleet Street, London EC4A 2HS.
© D. C. Thomson & Co., Ltd., 1996          **ISBN** 0-85116-626-1